THE INSPIRED EXECUTIVE

THE INSPIRED EXECUTIVE

The Art of Leadership

GRANVILLE N. TOOGOOD

CARROLL & GRAF PUBLISHERS, INC.
NEW YORK

First Carroll & Graf hardcover edition 1997
First Carroll & Graf trade paper edition 1999

Carroll & Graf Publishers, Inc.
19 West 21st Street
New York, NY 10010-6805

Library of Congress Cataloging-in-Publication Data is available.
ISBN: 0-7867-0579-5

Manufactured in the United States of America

Contents

Acknowledgments

I'd like to thank Matthew Cossolotto of Ovations International and Judy Glaser of Benchmark Communications for their very helpful anecdotal suggestions, and Jerry Gross for his fine eye and editing expertise.

Once again . . .
For Patricia, for Heather, and for Chase

What This Book Is About

We all meet competent, even talented people in business and life. But it's a curious paradox that you might never know they were competent or talented by listening to them talk. Most of us know someone who's got a special gift or skill that somehow never seems to take off. People languish. Lives languish. The years pass and we don't seem to go anywhere.

Lots of things get in the way of our winding trek to self-fulfillment: low self-confidence . . . shyness . . . a lack of drive . . . weak motivation . . . laziness . . . fear of failure . . . selfishness—you name it. The list is long. We find excuses why we are not what we should be. Yet we are amazed when lesser stars manage to shine more brightly. We watch in dismay and disbelief as the nerd from fifth grade rises to the top of the firm. We can hardly believe it when the creep from high school gets elected to Congress. And the jerk who couldn't even get into a fraternity in college marries a movie star and winds up running a Hollywood studio.

By contrast, the captain of the football team is in AA and selling insurance out of a storefront. The class president is doing time for securities fraud in a minimum-security prison, and the BMOC—the most popular guy in the school—died last year of a self-inflicted wound after failing to break into daytime TV.

What is happening here?

The nerd, the creep and the jerk rightly determined early on that they were at a significant disadvantage and resolved to compensate for their obvious lack of social graces and innate charm. All three wound up with more social grace and charm than anyone would have dreamed back in the dark days of school and college.

Not being given the gifts of life, they had to fashion those gifts for themselves. They began with brains. All three were smart. But had they relied only on their brains, they would never have met their potential. Instead, they *created* themselves in a new and better model—like butterflies emerging from the chrysalis. By the time they were done creating themselves they were almost unrecognizable to those who had known them before.

So in business, as in life, we sometimes have to remake ourselves. Most of us are trying, as the Army ad slogan says, to be all we can be. Only the army I'm talking about is in a forced march not notable for its military precision. Instead of snappy quick-stepping, most of us are misstepping. And all of us are occasionally stumbling as we lurch and grope our way through life from one goal to another.

It is in our most productive years that we come face to face with the greatest challenges of all: not only finding a job, but also finding the right one. Then not only keeping that job, but also advancing, even ascending to the top of the profession.

This is no easy task, as anyone who has ever earned a paycheck knows. But we have discovered what the critical factors in the success or failure of that epic journey are, and consequently we are in a position to take action that can smooth the nastiest bumps.

The most decisive factor is not our command of technology, or our understanding of the marketplace, or even our intelligence.

The most decisive factor is how other people see us.

How other people see us—and our ability to affect how they see us—are what makes most of us tick.

We're talking here about good, old-fashioned communications skills, what human resources people call "interpersonal skills." We're talking about that yucky soft stuff that hard-driving corporate powerhouses are often loath to discuss.

But it is exactly that soft stuff that makes or breaks us.

In the 1990s, PepsiCo set out to create the world's greatest executive development program. The objective was to develop outstanding leaders for future generations of senior management. PepsiCo put together a five-step process that taught seminar participants to: (1) think in different ways; (2) develop a point of view; (3) take that point of view on the road (sell it); (4) pull it all together; and (5) make it happen.

The best way to make it happen, according to PepsiCo chairman Roger Enrico, is to "communicate, communicate, communicate." Enrico himself taught parts of the seminar, using no props except for Martin Luther King, Jr.'s "I Have a Dream" speech.

"The point is not to make everyone an eloquent orator," he says, "but to show the power of communication."

In my book *The Articulate Executive: Learn to Look, Act, and Sound Like a Leader,* I provided communications fundamentals. In this book I talk about those fundamentals in a different way—Communications Value Added (CVA)—and how CVA can help anyone meet his or her potential in business or in life. *The Inspired Executive* is about the next step in communications, the step from theory to practice, from information to knowledge. As we plunge ahead in our swiftly changing world, knowledge forms into ideas, which translate into action. But somebody has to articulate those ideas before things begin to happen.

This book comes at a time when the world is shifting into another new age—the Age of Knowledge. The older Age of Information started winding down sometime around the demise of the mainframe computer. The Age of Knowledge was born about the time of the first personal computers. This is when knowledge was suddenly "at everyone's fingertips," as Bill Gates put it. For the first time, knowledge was available to anyone with a computer.

Whole eras are coming and going, emerging, overlapping, and fading right before our eyes. In my lifetime we have grown from the Industrial Age to the Age of the Atom to the Age of Information to the Age of the Service Economy. And now, whether we like it or not, we are setting sail into the still-uncharted but enormously rich and productive seas of the Age of Knowledge and its offspring, the knowledge industry.

Knowledge, and the ability to communicate that

knowledge, are the engines that will drive the twenty-first century. Today, economic reality is steering us toward professions that traffic exclusively in knowledge. Knowledge is already a capital asset. For example, in high-tech industries, products such as software, hardware, chips, new systems, devices and adapters are hitting obsolescence so rapidly that R&D and production cycles have shortened from years to months. No sooner is a new product out the factory door than it's becoming obsolete. But the growth of knowledge that went into the development of this blur of parading products holds its value and continues to expand, building measurable and competitive asset value as it grows. Knowledge of all kinds and in many disciplines becomes a valued commodity upon which industries, even economies, are built. (Your car, fitted with computer chips, is a "smart" car. Desert Storm was notable for its "smart" bombs.)

It is against this remarkable future that we contemplate the all-important human element. How are mere mortals to distinguish ourselves in such a technically sophisticated and intimidating new world?

The answer is: the same way we always have—by trying, with every available bit of help we can muster, to achieve our maximum performance potential. Paradoxically, with the "next wave" knowledge-based economy shifting like an earthquake beneath our feet, it will still fall to individual men and women to lead, coach, guide, instruct, enlighten, and teach. Without intelligent leadership the Age of Knowledge would be stillborn.

Computers govern our lives, and to a large degree our businesses as well. We are flying at Mach II into the unfathomable potential of the World Wide Web.

But computers can never lead us. We've got to lead ourselves. Computers—no matter how sophisticated—can never think for us. We must think for ourselves. The Age of Knowledge.

That's why CVA will help the people who will manage the Age of Knowledge.

CVA is the extra business that communications can bring to any transaction.

CVA is the decisive factor that can put a shaky deal over the top.

CVA is the difference between a lackluster presentation and a jolt of enlightenment and inspiration.

CVA is the glue that makes it possible for individuals and teams to operate more effectively in any work environment.

CVA can make a bland speech, an eye-opening event that will be remembered for years.

CVA is the necessary human element in an otherwise faceless interaction.

CVA is the component that can spell the difference between success and failure.

In other words, CVA is what it takes to make things happen.

Providing leaders with strong communications skills is the best way to make anything happen. But you don't have to be a leader to benefit. We all make things happen—

depending on our ability to inspire people, gain allies, and generate action.

The link between inspiration and action is us.

The fact is, the minute we open our mouths, people begin to size us up.

The Wall Street Journal reported that managers surveyed by the National Association of Colleges and Employers (NACE) rated "oral communications skills" the number one prerequisite to succeeding in the corporate promised land. Leadership skills ranked only sixth and computer skills last. Michael Forrest, executive director of NACE, noted that the top technical and consulting firms are hiring more liberal arts students—which underscores, he said, the importance of communications over "more transitory" technical skills.

The *Journal* also reported that interpersonal skills "have been a major factor in the success of managers and executives." The characteristics that propel us up the ladder—perfectionism, single-mindedness, and aggressiveness—"can trip us up as we near top management and have larger groups of people to manage," according to one consultant.

Almost everywhere we look we see that speaking skills (can you lead, defend your position, coach, inspire, motivate, captivate?) and interpersonal skills (are you comfortable, a good listener, sensitive, understanding, cordial, likable?) are evolving from soft intangibles to hard-core balance sheet assets.

That's what this book is about. It's one way you can fulfill your destiny and meet your highest potential in business. You *are* more than you think you are, and you *can be* more than you think you can be. You are your own best asset. All that you are or ever will be is already inside you. You need only mine that precious asset and start receiving the benefits.

Your actual potential, if you could somehow see it, would probably surprise you; it might even frighten you. Inside each of us sleeps a twin just waiting for an excuse to be born. This alter ego (picture a person of power and strength and character, a natural leader full of life and energy) can awaken and emerge—*but only at our invitation*.

Once your mysterious friend is out, you may never be the same.

It all comes down to who you can be.

In the end, your own words will determine how far you go.

Words are power—and you don't have to be a nerd to discover just how powerful they really are. The many ways you can use words constitute the hidden powers of CVA. And now more than ever—at the dawning of the Age of Knowledge—you and I and anyone else who expects to compete and advance can step up to a new level of effectiveness by seizing those powers for ourselves.

Read on.

CHAPTER
ONE

Communications Value Added (CVA)

Gilbert Rocci labored quietly for years in his cramped cubicle as an engineer for a midsize midwestern manufacturing company. His routine was predictable: Show up for work every day at 7:30 A.M., leave at 4:30 P.M. In between, he didn't talk much or pay attention to anything other than the assignment he was working on.

Gilbert Rocci was a worker bee. Industrious and dependable.

He would have gone on like that, happily buzzing away at his job day in and day out, had not something intervened that would change his life forever—forcing Gilbert to reinvent himself and become a new and better version of his old self.

One day his company decided to "re-engineer"—and Gilbert's comfortable routine was shattered. Gilbert was lucky. He got to keep his job. Because he was a good engineer with years of experience, his company's newly reorganized management asked him to cohead a new engineering and design "SWAT team" created to head off problems before products got to market.

A lucky break? A good move?

Most people would think so.

But instead of being delighted, Gilbert was terrified. He had never had to lead anything. He saw himself as shy, kind of a loner. He was good at solving problems, but he didn't feel comfortable in meetings. He talked to himself as he tried to solve problems at his computer, but he hated to speak publicly. The one time he presented a paper at a trade group convention he had been so boring people actually got up and walked out.

Gilbert knew he was trapped in a paradox of modern business life. He was competent, intelligent, talented. He loved his work. He'd always done the right thing—and now, suddenly, he felt lost, threatened, helpless. Now all his talent and know-how might be for naught if he was unable to communicate his ideas to others.

Panicked, Gilbert went to his human resources people and sought help. They recommended a professional counselor and coach who helped Gilbert find a large part of himself Gilbert didn't know existed.

Today, Gilbert is a changed man—so changed, in fact, that looking back, he hardly recognizes the man he used to be. Instead of fear and uncertainty, he's awash in excitement and self-confidence. Instead of experiencing anxiety when he has to speak, he now looks forward to every opportunity to inform and inspire. Instead of feeling dread at the prospect of presenting himself to others, he now actually enjoys himself.

And the more he speaks, the more fun he has.

The more fun he has, the more he helps others and the more he helps himself.

His "new man" image has paid off in other ways. He's been tapped to head the entire engineering function, and there's even talk he'll be invited to join the senior management committee.

But the greatest benefit has gone to all the people who work with Gilbert. They see him as a leader. He delivers important messages. He defines problems and details solutions. He empowers. He's gone from sitting unnoticed on the bench to coaching the whole team. *And he is a good coach.* He brings all his old expertise to the playing field, but while he is still a good scientist, now he is something more. Gilbert's latent talent for leadership has ignited, and everyone benefits.

All this good has come to pass because one person woke up, reached up, looked around for the first time, and started stretching.

Audiences will decide within eight seconds if you are worth listening to.

The new business environment we all work in is full of Gilberts and people like him: people who walk around never recognizing that they carry within themselves another person who is longing to get out. It is almost impossible to measure the potential that this "superself" brings to our lives, our careers, and the organizations for which we labor. But we do know that the potential is real, and the sooner we activate that potential, the better. The name of that potential is CVA, about which I will have more to say in a moment.

But first let's go back to the defining event of the 1980s.

After the crash of 1987 and subsequent restructuring of corporate America—and in the eerie silence following the collapse of a financial empire ruled by self-styled masters of the universe—academics, consultants, and gurus of every stripe descended upon dazed corporate survivors who were trying to grope their way through a radically changed marketplace. Just about anyone with a new idea and an acronym, or an old idea made to look new, was greeted as a sage or a savior.

No one had a clue how to revive the faltering economy—but almost everyone had an idea.

That's how we got downsizing, process reengineering, total quality, best practices, continuous improvement, speed, benchmarking, delayering, just-in-time inventory, cross-functional teams, empowerment, boundarylessness (a big GE favorite), common vision, entrepreneurism, globalization, and all the rest.

Then on top of all that, somebody told us about Economic Value Added (EVA). They said it was a new way to gauge financial performance. Simply put, EVA is a company's net operating profit after taxes—and after taking out an elusive element called the true cost of capital. To me, that sounds like another way of saying that if you lower costs, you increase productivity.

Almost every CEO in America fell in love with EVA.

Then, just when we thought we had a handle on value added (consultant talk) or added value (the rest of us talk), somebody else decided to present us with yet another "added"—Market Value Added (MVA).

Market Value Added is the difference between what investors put into a company and what they take out. But to me, MVA is something else. To me, Market Value Added is when you figure out your core competency, then pour all your resources into selling what you do best. Market Value Added is also what happens when a leader sees the light and acts wisely. Robert Goizueta of Coca-Cola saw that Coke was the world's most recognizable brand name, so he killed "New Coke" and concentrated on strengthening an already effervescent franchise. Jack Welch saw that you don't get anywhere in business unless you're No. 1 or No. 2, so he jettisoned GE's poor performers, beefed up financial services (GE Capital), and led GE on a charge to higher profits. Philip Morris saw that cigarettes were a winner worldwide, so it separated tobacco from food and marketed Marlboro into a powerhouse brand name, second only to Coke.

Market Value Added, like Economic Value Added, is good for investors. Places such as Coca-Cola and GE, which pack a two-punch EVA and MVA wallop, have consistently seen their share prices rise and their shareholders cheer.

Then, of course, if you've traveled in Europe lately there's another value added—the Value Added Tax.

Now, in case you still feel "added" challenged, I'm going to drag one more "added" out onto the playing field. This idea I propose to call Communications Value Added (CVA).

CVA says basically that what you say and how you say it can determine the success of your business. Also, if you're good with EVA and MVA, you'll be twice as good with CVA. And if you're good with CVA, you'll go a long way toward fulfilling your potential.

CVA works for people who are in the process of learning how to position themselves as leaders in their organizations, people who should be harnessing the power of their potential early in their careers. We are also talking about people who already lead their organizations: CEOs, presidents, COOs, CFOs—anyone in business to whom others turn for guidance. And for all those who don't happen to be pursuing careers, CVA is as true in life as it is in business.

CVA states that what you say and how you say it can determine the success of your business.

Rule: If a leader with good business sense or a great idea can talk the talk—charm Wall Street, inspire employees, reassure shareholders, manipulate the press to good advantage, win friends and influence people—the company and the individual will fare better. In fact, a company can fare so well on the communications skills of the CEO alone that the outcome will be not only measurable but actually amazing.

> **Remember the *18-Minute Wall*. That's the maximum amount of time people can listen to someone talk.**

Consider the surprising result of an as yet unpublished Yankelovich study for *Fortune* magazine, which found that blue chip companies with highly visible CEOs and superior reputations (the link between the two is essential to the study's findings) had P/E (price–earnings) ratios averaging 50 percent above blue chips with weaker reputations but similar assets (in other words, less visible leaders incapable of talking the talk). Jim Taylor, former executive vice president of Hill & Knowlton and onetime Yankelovich president, says the study reveals that a company's rep is driven by its CEO's rep, and that the CEO's rep is a balance sheet asset—often measured in the hundreds of millions of dollars.

CVA is a revenue-producing business function like operations, manufacturing, or distribution. Only it costs a lot less and is immediately available to everyone, regardless of his or her level or rank within the organization.

But it is most effective and visible when the people at

the top enthusiastically practice CVA with such skill they become one with their brand names.

For example, Goizueta and Welch—especially Welch—are inseparable from the identities and very souls of their companies.

Welch, who grew up with a nagging stutter, is a man possessed when he exhorts his troops. All traces of stutter evaporate in the heat of his convictions as he describes his visions, plans, and strategies—rolling over his audiences like a juggernaut of ideas. Welch is not a big man. But his eyes are alive with intelligence and excitement, and when he gets into one of his memorable "locker room" pep talks, he looms as large as any coach in the NFL.

> **Great speakers are inseparable from their messages.**

Welch pushes hard for speed and productivity, talking about "boundarylessness," "workouts," "stretch targets," and other catalysts he loves to lob into the GE mix to generate productive change. The standards he sets are so high—*"Looney Toons* stuff that he has no right to ask," according to Steven Kerr, GE's vice president for corporate leadership development—that a reasonable person might expect reactions of trepidation and disbelief from the audience. But Welch, borne high by the passions of his beliefs, is so charismatic that "they get energized," Kerr says. "They don't know what part they're going to play, but they are going to damned well help him do whatever he asks." At the end of a speech, Welch exhorts a group: "This is the message. Go home and tell your people."

That's CVA.

Is there life at GE after Jack? That's a question one hears not only inside the company, but also on Wall Street every day. The answer, of course, is yes. But Welch's successor has to bring more than competency and desire to the job. That person will have to look, act, and sound like a leader if GE is to continue to enjoy those attractive P/Es.

In a *Fortune* magazine interview, Welch talked about his successor: "I want somebody with incredible energy who can excite others, who can define their vision, who finds change fun and doesn't get paralyzed by it," he said. "I want somebody who feels comfortable in Delhi or Denver. I mean, somebody who really feels comfortable and can talk to all kinds of people."

If you suddenly pull CVA out of a company that has for years enjoyed a rich CVA harvest, the results can be shocking.

When Lee Iacocca left Chrysler, for example, his corporate face and voice disappeared from radio, television, magazines, and newspapers. Overnight, the perception of momentum at Chrysler he had built over the years was weakened. It lost its voice, its vision, its character—even its personality. The company itself seemed to falter, and didn't start getting back into high gear until the middle '90s.

When Intel suffered a setback with its famed Pentium chip, it was CEO Andy Grove who reassured Wall Street that the problem was a laughably insignificant burp at a very big banquet. Intel went on to thrive—even in the face of distant but ominous threats from the World Wide Web that could have collapsed the market for this chip.

And when the Web abruptly loomed large on Microsoft's cloudless horizon, the first person to spot the storm clouds was Bill Gates, who immediately began telling his people to focus on info highway applications. Gates convinced worried analysts and other skeptics that, no, the sky was not falling . . . that Microsoft had anticipated the Web . . . and that the future looked as bright as ever. What he said was: Everybody relax. I'm in control. Everything is going to be all right.

We believed him—and all may yet be right with Microsoft. Bill Gates seems set to convert the problem of the World Wide Web into a Microsoft solution.

At a recent analysts meeting I watched the CEO of a telecommunications company turn an opportunity to inform, excite, and inspire into just another predictable exercise in boredom. An analysts meeting is a forum where CVA can produce quick results. But this poor fellow was either unable to rise to the occasion, hobbled by inept handlers, shackled to a lifeless text, or lacking in vision. His humdrum presentation—read right off the page and apparently written by a clueless apparatchnik—went on so long that people were taking comfort in their *Wall Street Journals*, holding their heads in their hands, or—if they happened to be among the lucky few near a door—ducking out the exits.

If you do your job right—if you unleash the CVA—the stock price is supposed to go up. But his stock price plunged two points—a drop that slashed the company's market value by 17 percent. Curiously, if you read the CEO's prepared text, there is good news. But good news apparently counts for little if the CEO can't cut it in front of an important audience. My bet is that if this CEO had come across as a leader, the stock would have gone up rather than down two points.

After all, this guy had the basic skills. He was once a pretty good consultant, understood the business, had a grasp of the numbers. All that was missing was the most important part—the ability to inspire confidence. His mistake was his willingness to settle for mediocrity—to simply show up and read someone else's speech. Somebody should have told him that those precious minutes he blew were actually worth tens of millions of dollars. For a tiny window of eighteen minutes of speaking, that's a whole lot of productivity. Not bad for a few moments' work.

That's CVA.

Gilbert Rocci—the engineer who found the CVA within himself—inspires his fellow workers to new heights of excellence and productivity.

That's CVA.

In the right place at the right time, CVA can produce explosive results. A young man who had invented a new portable security device was unable to interest venture capitalists in his product—until he and a friend financed the production of several thousand of the gadgets themselves—then wrangled an appearance on QVC television to personally market the product. The young man spoke with conviction and confidence as he demonstrated how the alarm worked. The entire stock sold out in fewer than ten minutes—and serious investors started knocking on the door the next day.

That's CVA.

Remington Electric Shavers went from a close shave with bankruptcy to a household name with the help of the company's owner, Victor Kiam, who served as Remington's on-air spokesperson for years.

That's CVA.

Sy Syms speaks like a Harvard don as he hawks his bargain-basement garments. He parlays his minor celebrity and smooth voice into a booming business in the New York area.

That's CVA.

A man called David Orrick enthusiastically pitches his industrial-strength vacuum cleaners on the radio and cleans up big time.

That's CVA.

Mort Lebenthal increased his bond trading firm's business fivefold by churning out cloying, pseudo-folksy, highly irritating commercials on radio and TV that somehow got people to think Lebenthal was the answer to their future financial security.

This, too, is CVA.

The characteristics of leadership are complex, elusive.

But acknowledged leaders exhibit certain recognizable assets, which I have bunched, for purposes of easy retention, into a profile I call the Hi-C's.

The Hi-C's help paint a picture of what we're looking for when we talk about CVA. To understand what the Hi-C's are and how they flesh out and overlap with the idea of CVA, look at this:

The HI-C's
Communications Value Added (CVA)

HOT	NOT
Conviction	Uncertainty
Communication	Alienation
Concentration	Absentmindedness
Clarity	Fuzziness
Consistency	Confusion
Continuity	Discontinuity
Character	Lack of character
Creativity	Mediocrity
Credibility	Doubt
Candor	Artifice
Competence	Incompetence
Coolness	Fear
Cohesion	Sloppiness
Concept	Emptiness
Color	Drabness
Crispness	Blather
Civility	Boorishness
Caring	Indifference

You'll never remember all that—and you don't have to. But it's enough to know that conviction is better than uncertainty, communication is better than alienation; creativity is better than mediocrity; and clarity, consistency, and continuity are better than fuzziness, uncertainty, and discontinuity.

It is arguably true that we are the best spokesperson for ourselves, whether we run a business, own one, or work in one. If we speak up, we can be heard. We can make a difference. But if we turn away and remain silent—even when we know we should stand and be counted—the only thing about which we can be absolutely certain is that we will have forfeited our opportunity to affect the course of events. Instead, we may wind up at the mercy of whatever the winds of chance bring our way.

> **Excellent speakers transform the complex to the comprehensible.**

The Seven Principles
of CVA

The first principle of CVA is always be interesting—never bore. This would seem like an obvious admonition. But it amazes me how many people ignore this fundamental guideline—and it is even more remarkable how few people in business view it as necessary. But if you fail to elicit interest from your audience, all your preparations and efforts are doomed.

I can think of countless ways to be more interesting. Here are a few:

- *Begin strongly.* Engage your audience in the first eight seconds (that's how long it takes for people to size you up and decide whether they want to listen to you). You can try starting with a personal story, or an anecdote (something you may have read about, for example), or a rhetorical question (What is the single greatest challenge facing our business in the next five years?). You could also try beginning with the ending (hit them with the point, the bottom line right up front and right between the eyes), or a pertinent quotation from a famous person (sometimes a little cutesy). Or you might begin with a projection into the future ("Fifteen years from now the business we all take for granted will be very different . . ."), or a look into the past to show how things have changed ("Thirty years ago if you wanted to buy a . . ."), or maybe even a stab at humor (watch out—when people try to be funny it often falls flat because the humor comes across as sarcasm, or inappropriate, or poorly told, or the speaker bungles the punch line and fails to tie the joke to a business point).

Whatever you do, make certain that you link your story or anecdote to a specific business point you want to make. For example, if you start by telling your audience a little story of a particularly bad experience you had at a restaurant, you need to link that story to the general message of your talk, which might be the constant need for improved service in your business.

The second principle of CVA is always provide something extra, something of value, something memorable to every audience. This may mean taking a position—even though you may not have realized you had a point of view buried in all those data. Or it could mean teaching the audience something they could not have known until they heard you speak—even though when you began preparing your presentation you may not have realized you had anything to teach.

My message here is that you can add measurable value to any presentation simply by taking the time to figure out what the hidden message or hidden teaching is—and then exhibiting that message for all to see. For example, you're making a quarterly presentation to your senior management about the progress of a specific project. Typically, you might just give an update and throw out a few numbers. But suppose those numbers are telling you something interesting. Suppose you notice that market share on the East Coast is down. Is this just an anomaly? You check it out and discover that drivers for one of your distributors have been staging spot slowdowns. Product is not getting to store shelves, and the competition, which uses another distributor, is having a field day. A further investigation uncovers other, even more serious problems.

You think about your presentation and in the end you wind up with a completely different approach. Instead of being the predictable update, your reworked presentation evolves into an important wake-up call for management: We're vulnerable on important fronts for different reasons—and we've already started making a series of changes to head off future problems.

The third principle of CVA is always be master of your presentation—never allow your presentation to master you. Three important rules are adjuncts to this principle.

1. Always begin and end your presentation with just you talking. Do not put up a slide or overhead (sometimes a corporate logo is unavoidable, and that's all right). But

19

stay away from headline slides and agendas. Instead, start strongly (see principle 1) and end strongly.

2. Use only graphics, schematics, tables, illustrations, or photographs—try hard to avoid using word slides. Most people believe word slides double their effectiveness and provide reinforcement. That's wrong. Word slides slash your effectiveness to almost zero and create redundancy (people can't pay attention to you while they're trying to read something). Note: Keep your word slides for your own use as notes or to hand out to your audience—but *only after* your presentation.

3. Introduce your next slide while the old slide is still on the screen. What I mean by this is, don't do what everybody else does—put up a slide and then start talking to that slide the moment it appears. Instead, prepare what I call a "roll-in"—an eight- to twenty-second summary of what the next slide says before you actually show the next slide. In this way, audiences will recognize that you are in control of your own presentation. This is important if you want to be seen as a leader.

> **Introduce your next slide while the current slide is still on the screen.**

For example, you're talking about new productivity initiatives, and a slide showing a graphic of productivity trend lines is on the screen. Normally, you might finish talking about productivity gains, then switch to the next slide showing, say, revenue gains tied to productivity. When the revenue slide goes up, most people would typically start talking about revenue. But I'm suggesting that you "bridge" to the revenue slide while the program slide is still up. You might say something like, "That productivity is reflected in revenue gains of more than 12 percent in operations, 15 percent in manufacturing, and more than 20 percent in our affiliates—as you can see here. . . ." *Then* you hit the button—and only then does the revenue slide appear. This is a person who obviously doesn't have to rely on a slide show to know what to say. This is a person who clearly is not giving someone else's presentation. This is a person who has command of his subject, of his presentation, and therefore of his audience.

Never begin or end your presentation with slides or overheads.

The fourth principle of CVA is to speak only about what you know. Too often people accept invitations to speak, then discover they have agreed to talk on a subject they are not competent to discuss. For example, a friend of mine who teaches history and political science at a university agreed to talk about economic change in emerging nations. He came away from that experience a changed man. Later, he told me that it had never occurred to him *not* to talk about the subject his hosts had requested. But he found himself struggling with the assignment, then

gave the speech with reservations and a lack of depth—
and it showed. He did not bomb, but neither he nor his
audience came away from the experience satisfied.

The lesson here is to stick to your knitting. If his hosts
wanted to hear about economic change in emerging countries, they probably should have asked someone else. By
the same token—and more importantly—my friend
should have used a little common sense and given them
a choice: He would be happy to speak on a subject he
knew well—the agonizing birth pangs of democracy in
Russia and the threat of a relapse to communism, for example. Otherwise, they'd do better to find an expert on
economic change in emerging nations.

**If you expect people to listen, talk only about what
you know.**

---

*The fifth principle of CVA is always to be sensitive to
the needs of your audience.* For example, never make an
audience of busy people such as senior corporate officers
sit and wait for you to get to your point.

Nothing makes businesspeople more impatient than
the creeping suspicion that the time they are giving to the
speaker is not time well spent. Second, always try to anticipate exactly what your audience wants to hear. Do
these people want just the quarterly numbers? Or do they
want you to reassure them, step by step, that the project
they have invested in so heavily is not a waste of money?
Do they want to hear the details of yesterday's deal, or

want to know why they should agree to go ahead with the new transaction?

At another level, are they interested in what you have to say or how you say it? For instance, does the board really care about product X, or are they sizing you up for promotion? Are conventioneers interested in hearing the studio exec talk about the financial and accounting acrobatics that go into making movies, or would they prefer to hear war stories and scuttlebutt about stars from a Hollywood insider? Would an audience of business leaders prefer to hear about the finer points of Middle East diplomacy, or revealing anecdotes about big names on the world stage from a famous former statesman? Human nature will always demand the latter—make no mistake. And remember that audiences always prefer the brief, crisp, and well-packaged to the long and mushy.

> **If you try to force a smile, you may wind up looking like you just stepped on a nail.**

The sixth principle of CVA is to speak in pictures. Use anecdotes, analogies, illustrations, and hard facts. We live in a time when almost everyone you meet will have been brought up on a heavy diet of TV (today the *average* TV viewing time per person per day is six hours). Since you are not a television set, you will have to compensate for that deficiency by making a point of speaking in anecdotes whenever possible. We're also conditioned by a heavy cultural addiction to computers and computer games as well—especially among younger people. So the cards are stacked against the speaker who fails to recognize that simple concept. Vague notions, general ideas, and abstractions, no matter how worthy or noble, just can't cut it. If you measure your success with an audience on whether people enjoy listening to what you have to say and remember what you said days—even weeks—later, then you can't rely on mere concept. If you seek good productivity for your audience as well as for yourself, you've got to throw in lots of anecdotal evidence. That's the fun part of any talking and the fun part of listening.

You must remember that each time you tell a story or give an example, that story or example has got to be linked to your theme, your message.

Do this and you need never worry about whether you will succeed with your audience. Not only will you succeed, you may even triumph. Throughout history it is the storytellers who have taught us and led us. This last point takes me to my seventh, and final principle.

Always speak in word pictures.

The seventh principle of CVA is PREPARATION. A minimum amount of preparation can yield maximum results, especially if the planning and design of your speech or presentation adhere to five simple components: strong start, one theme, vivid examples, conversational language, and strong ending. Preparation usually means tighter, crisper, briefer—all of which are good. Preparation also means clearer message, higher interest factor, greater depth, longer retention, more fun for speaker and listener alike, and overall a much higher level of quality.

Great speeches share five key characteristics: strong start, one theme, vivid examples, conversational language, and strong ending.

CHAPTER

THREE

Business Likability: The Keys to the Kingdom

Cynthia Wachsman is a hit with her customers but bombs with her family. She's alienated her kids and is contemplating divorce.

Bob Gaines has a lot of friends at work and is in line for the top job. But outside work he's a loner and doesn't have many social friends.

Harold Watts, on the other hand, is hard to like even on a good day. He's humorless, socially inept, sometimes withdrawn, and moody. But put him in front of an audience and he becomes another person: crisp, interesting, articulate, on top of his subject.

Jack Finley is a nerdy kind of guy—the kind of harmless person you wouldn't notice on the street or spend time talking to at a cocktail party. But he's a brilliant strategist and comes alive when you get him on his area of expertise.

Cynthia, Bob, Harold, and Jack—and tens of

thousands of people like them—all have one thing in common: an elusive but potent phenomenon I call business likability.

Paradoxically, likability and business likability are not the same thing. Business likability is the invisible measurement that determines whether people will be willing to accept us as leaders in our businesses.

For example, Tom Waitley is loved by almost everyone who knows him at work, at play, or at home. He's definitely likable. In fact, he oozes likability—yet he has never managed to break into top management. The reason: Likability by itself is not enough. You've got to know how to put your likability to work. When you do that, you've jumped to the profitable level of business likability.

Take the case of an investment adviser I know who wanted to expand her client base. Her focus was superior service. Her objective was higher revenues. Her message was: We must be willing to change our investment policy today if we expect to retire comfortably tomorrow. So she set up a series of free seminars to outline her strategies, sent out invitations, and then used all her powers of persuasion to win new business.

Her business ballooned—and today she's a money manager who heads her own firm.

It was more than just competency that got her where she is today. She's made it to the top of her profession because she looks like she's having *fun*.

Focus and fun. Together, they can generate business likability.

These are aspects of CVA.

Once you wrap your mind around your message, you can begin to be yourself. If you are sincere, the audience will relax and listen; you're on your way. Once you're on your way you can enjoy yourself. (But don't make the mistake of taking your eye off the ball—trying to tell us more than we have to know or explain a lot of irrelevant numbers for example—because then your heart isn't in the right place, and you might be knocked off track.)

> **People will want to do business with you if you look and sound like you're having fun in your work.**

Business likability, once acquired, is priceless. It's a state of mind—and it counts in every transaction. In the end, business likability is not *how* the deal is done, but *why*. Without business likability, often there is no deal.

William Branson, the genial British tycoon and chairman of Virgin Atlantic Airways, is a one-time hippie child of the '60s who built his easy likability into a business empire. Business partners and customers alike find comfort in this nonthreatening, long-haired, ever-smiling man who sometimes holds court cross-legged on the floor of his London office. He has a reputation for being community-minded, environmentally friendly, generous in his transactions, and honest. That's likability. But he's also focused, intelligent, articulate, and full of a sense of fun. He advocates excitement, creativity, and adventure on the job. That's business likability. It has a lot more to do with the gut and the heart than the head.

While our conscious mind (let's call this individual Professional Person) is trying to listen to what we're saying, the real decision-maker, our unconscious mind (let's call this individual Primal Person) is checking us out from top to bottom. Primal Person can figure out in seconds whether we are worthy of even one more moment of his time and continued interest. In other words, Primal Person calls the shots. Once Primal Person has spoken, the deal is either done or undone.

While Professional Person is still trying to listen, Primal Person has heard enough and has already made up his mind. Professional Person picks up words like chopsticks, discretely assembling grains of rice. Primal Person wolfs down the whole meal in huge bites. Professional Person is listening with his ears and using his mind to reflect on concept. Primal Person is listening with his gut and using his heart to form impressions.

And Primal Person, it should be noted, is not always radar-scanning just for warm and fuzzy.

Primal Person is also probing for business likability, expressed in intelligence, ambition, analytical skills, and marketing talent. "Warm and fuzzy," even humor, may have nothing to do with it. A soft-spoken, introverted accountant can show surprising business likability simply by being himself and speaking plainly. In fact, a frank lack of acting or drama of any kind can be refreshing—*as long as what you say is interesting and as long as you are interested in what you are saying*.

But to achieve business likability you've got to have

your audience's interests at heart—ahead of your own. Serve your audience well, and your interests will follow. If I'm in the audience and you seem to sincerely care about what you're saying, seem to care about *me*, then I may find myself liking you—even though I may not agree with you. It is far more important that I like you than that I agree with you. If I like you and disagree with you, I respect you and we still have some basis to enter into a working relationship. If I don't like you, but do agree, that relationship is less likely. But if I don't like you and don't agree with you, we have nothing.

So pitch to clients and prospective clients with a genuine desire to help *them*. Turn down business in the short run if it's better for your client (which will eventually pay off for you in the long run). Be generous with your time and advice; protect the interests of your client.

This is not a new idea, but it's surprising how few people abide by it. Veteran New York public relations wizard William Ruder had so much work that he frequently had to turn business away, and at one point was trying to reduce the size of his business. I asked him to tell me the secret of his success.

His answer was to the point. Without hesitation he said, "Serve your clients well, and your clients will serve you." Bill's selflessness, together with his talent, honest guidance, and good advice, made him well liked in the corporate world. His likability translated into revenues and success.

The secret to Bill's business *was* his likability. No one

doubted whether he cared. When he spoke, people listened because he had likability. They acted on what he said because he had business likability.

Make what you say interesting and be interested in what you say.

People with a high business likability quotient also have a knack for anticipating customer needs. To do that, you've got to have a talent for recognizing change, then a willingness to capitalize on historical shifts while they're still in progress. For example, a friend of mine who retired from IBM admitted privately that for years he sold machines "that people didn't want, didn't need, and couldn't afford."

Maybe that's why, about the time he was retiring, customers the world over finally caught on and decided that they didn't want vendors like my friend anymore. What they wanted was a mutually productive, long-term working relationship. They wanted someone who would look after them, someone they could trust, someone who could help them get quality, speed, better productivity, and solutions to problems.

Customers decided that what they really needed was a partner.

Once they realized that they were looking for a partner instead of a salesperson, the question of whom they chose to be their partner came down to one simple concept.

> **Customers want someone to look after them and provide solutions.**

Business likability.

They wanted competence, commitment, and character—but above all they needed business likability. And that's when my friend from IBM reinvented himself and began a new life as a consultant. He's got a small stable of big clients and today he's happier and earning more than ever before.

We've all seen business likability at work: There's the senior exec who takes off his jacket, rolls up his sleeves, forgoes the lectern, and walks to the front of the stage to *have a conversation* with his employees. He's not making a speech. He's talking to us as if he knows us personally. And he's telling stories that not only make the business point but also are fun to listen to. So we (1) pay attention; (2) remember later what was said; and (3) come away having a good feeling about the guy. That's good for the guy, good for us, and good for the business—because it makes us all feel as if we belong, as if we matter.

Then, of course, there's the pitch in the conference room. We listen to two excruciatingly boring presentations that take up most of the morning, and now here comes this guy who makes us all sit up and listen. This guy knows his stuff. He uses few visual aids, but he's captivating: He's animated, comfortable, conversational, and anecdotal all at the same time. You could say he's *colorful*. His presentation looks and sounds a lot different from the others.

It's a lot shorter, too, and more interesting—and he's done an effective job of making his point.

Without business likability you could be the smartest, most competent, most determined worker in your company but still wind up short of your potential and unable to fulfill your promise. You might not get the order, or the assignment, or the promotion, or the raise. You might not even get to keep your job. Opportunity may pass you by, fortune fall between the cracks. You see good things gravitate toward other people.

By contrast, if you've got business likability, good things—a lot of good things—seem to go your way.

So two questions arise:

What is the nature of business likability? And if you suspect you may not have it, how do you get it?

To answer question 1, think about people you know or have seen in business who are smart and competent but don't seem to come across well. What do these people lack?

When you think about it, they seem to share certain unproductive characteristics. For example, they:

• tend to be boring—especially in their presentations, speeches, and even in meetings;

• seem incapable of positioning themselves as leaders;

• often suffer an unflattering personality change when asked to speak or present information;

• take too long trying to tell us too much and wind up telling us almost nothing.

There's more, but you get the picture.

If you see yourself in any portion of this portrait, take heart, because we are all guilty of these missteps to one degree or another. Yet, happily, the solution is a simple quick fix for most of us—which is to say that even if you do not see yourself as a leader, you can *still teach yourself* the *characteristics of leadership!*

And importantly, you need not be liked socially to have business likability. In fact, you can expect some people to be personally indifferent toward you in a business as well as a social setting. But at the same time, you can enhance your business likability. So while I might not want to spend hours with you in a bar or at a party (or vice versa), the part of me that is Primal Person has decided that you are the person with whom I want to do business.

This leads us to the second question. What are the characteristics that position us as leaders and get us closer to the action and transaction?

First, the person with whom I want to do business is interesting. He or she grabs my attention with unexpected behavior that raises communication to a new level. For example, she engages my mind right off the bat with a personal story, anecdote, conclusion, recommendation, rhetorical question, projection, or even humor.

Second, he makes it very clear early on what his point is, why he's speaking, why I should listen.

Third, he doesn't rely on a single simple concept to carry the day. Rather, he convinces me with anecdotal proof and support to back up his point—like a lawyer giving evidence in court.

Fourth, she's conversational. She doesn't sound like a businesswoman. She sounds more like a friend. She's not trying to impress me with "secret handshake" language or buzzwords to show me how brilliant she is.

Fifth, she takes a position, has a point of view. She's not just rattling off a laundry list or a string of chronological events. She sees a business point in everything she says; everything she says is tied to her message. And her message has a very definite point of view.

Sixth, he's relaxed. He's comfortable with his job, with his subject, with himself. He does not appear to be acting a role, and has no trouble putting everyone else at ease— because he himself is at ease.

Seventh, I notice that he appears to govern his presentation. His presentation does not govern him. He begins without any props or visual aids, and he ends the same way. What few visual aids he does use are all simple graphics, and they all support his message. There's not a single word slide in the lot.

Eighth, she introduces the next slide while the current slide is still on the screen. She uses the pictures to back up her points. She is *not* using the pictures as a script to tell her what she is supposed to say next. She is leading the show. The show is not leading her.

As if those weren't enough, she gets the job done in

less than half the time it would take the next guy to do the same presentation.

Finally, she never speaks with her eyes down. She's almost always looking right at us when she's pressing her message and driving home her points.

There's a lot to like.

I'm impressed—and by the time he or she is done talking I almost want to stand up and applaud. At the very least, I want to give that person some business.

The magical bit of alchemy that has transpired here is testimony to the power of business likability. Hundreds of people every day enjoy the fruits of likability; so can you. You need only remember the nine landmarks on the journey to making your own likability come alive:

1　Be interesting.

2　Get to your point quickly.

3　Give examples to back up your point.

4　Be conversational.

5　Take a position.

6　Relax.

7　Govern your presentation—don't let it govern you.

8　Look at people when you talk.

9　Be crisp.

So if you are intelligent, competent, and right-minded about your career and your business, yet still seem unable to scale walls of resistance or to make things happen, you need to cultivate more business likability.

Work to establish business likability in your working relationships. That's your foundation. Then, as Bill Ruder said earlier, serve your client and you serve yourself. Serve your audience and you serve yourself.

These are the characteristics of CVA that will make it possible to parlay your talents into growth, productivity, enhanced revenues—and more fun that you may ever have thought you deserved from your work.

Great leaders are also great teachers. If you meet a great leader, you will come away feeling you have learned something of value.

CHAPTER
FOUR

The Surprising Power of Words

When you talk about CVA, you're talking about word power.

I remember as a child being persuaded to change my opinion of a friend by another kid who poisoned my mind with words of bile and contempt. It never occurred to me that my ten-year-old pal Chris was anything other than an all-around good guy—until supercool Carl Shepherd persuaded me that Chris was a loser. Carl kept referring to Chris as a creep and a jerk and talked me into ditching Chris as my friend and hanging out with Carl and his buddies. Too late, I found out that Carl and company were the real losers—but by then I'd been kicked out of Carl's gang and wound up for a while with no friends.

Chris went on to be a Rhodes scholar and Carl eventually did jail time for auto theft. Years later, I still regret that I let Carl turn my head. The kid was wrong, and I was wrong to allow myself to be swayed—but to this day I am amazed by the power of words to persuade.

I can remember countless times when comforting words brought me back from the edge of sadness, fear, or grief. Broken love, cruel death, painful longing—all lulled by gentle words that somehow kissed the psychic wound and made it better, the roaring lion of anguish made to lie down and sleep for a while.

As a teenager I remember I thought my world had come to an end when the most beautiful girl I had ever seen allowed me to date her a couple of times—and then, just when I was intoxicated with love and passion, dumped me like a half-eaten sandwich. I never thought I would know that pain of rejection. I was overwhelmed with the power of it, and it took kind and understanding words from my mom to get me over it.

And when my mother died twenty years later and I experienced real grief, I drew comfort and inspiration from a book of spiritual wisdom given me by an old friend. I remember reading that "death is like taking off a tight shoe" and "opening the doors of a smoke-filled room and stepping into the sunlight and fresh air." At the time, those words themselves were like fresh air.

I also remember being astonished how a few well-chosen words could dash my dreams or make me wild with anticipation.

"Never," "no," and "absolutely not" were missiles that pierced my dreams. On the other hand, reading clever ad copy about a new movie or new book stoked my interest to the point of purchase.

Words have the power to heal or to kill. Give a scalpel to an insane man and he could slash you to ribbons. Put the same scalpel in the hands of an accomplished surgeon and he could save your life.

I heard a story about an obese boy of fifteen who was so anguished by the unkind words of his classmates that one day he walked into class and announced, "I can't take it anymore," and shot himself dead in front of his tormentors.

I heard another story of a little girl who lay in a coma after being hit by a car. Doctors held out little hope. They said she could not recover and told the parents to prepare for the worst.

But the parents refused to accept that their daughter was doomed. Instead, they sat by her hospital bed, touching her, taking turns holding her hand, whispering words of encouragement and love day and night, never leaving her side. On the fifth day, the child suddenly woke up, saying she had been in "another place" but had been able to hear and understand her parents—even though her body had been unconscious. She said that she had been drawn to "a beautiful light with Jesus in it" but had decided to go back to her parents when she heard their words of love.

If you're in the dark, a few words at the right time can shed light on the path ahead. A friend of mine had no idea, as a college senior, what he wanted to do with his life—until one day he attended a lecture given by a surgeon. The doctor talked about the enormous gratification he had gotten from his work, and told about several remarkable cases in which patients' lives had been saved. These stories of hope so inspired my friend that he set out to become a doctor himself. Today he's a successful eye surgeon on the West Coast.

Three minutes with the right audience can be worth a year at your desk.

Words make us what we are, and words make the dead come back to life.

History is alive with the voices of our forefathers. We have castles in Spain, ruins in Rome, and cathedrals all across the rolling hills of Central Europe. But they all pale in comparison with the mountains of oral and written history that evoke the ghosts of ages long gone. Through the eyes and ears of people who have gone before we hear the slap of sandals on the streets of Sparta, recoil to the clang of iron and the thunder of horses as Roman armies rumble across the ancient world, watch and listen as Christ speaks to the children of Galilee.

Emerging from all that clamor and all those distant words are the voices of people, once living, who shaped the world we know today. They are gone, but their words live on—and give us a tiny glimpse of the worlds they knew.

Picture Queen Elizabeth I, Henry VIII's only surviving child, riding on horseback to the head of her army as the Spanish Armada approaches England in 1588. Philip II of Spain, one of Elizabeth's spurned suitors, has sent the "invincible" fleet against Protestant England. The future of the country hangs in the balance.

Elizabeth sits straight in the saddle and speaks to her troops.

"My loving people!" she shouts. "Let tyrants fear!"

In a language of another age, she prepares to lead her army in battle: "I am come among you at this time . . . to live or die . . . to lay down, for my God and for my kingdom and for my people, my honor and my blood. . . ."

Pulling herself higher in the saddle, eyes blazing, she cries out: "I know I have the body of a weak and feeble woman. But I have the heart of a king!"

She proudly defies the king of Spain, then promises "a famous victory over the enemies of my God, of my kingdom, and of my people."

These are the fighting words of one of the strongest women in history. We know from chronicles of the day that her subjects loved and feared their flinty queen, and that if the Spanish Armada had not failed, her words to her army probably would have spurred great deeds on the battlefield. But as it turned out, fortune did not smile on the armada—much of which wound up wrecked on rocks in a terrible storm. But Elizabeth's words defined the character of England—proud, defiant, resolute. This was sixteenth-century CVA at its best.

In the mid-twentieth century, World War II brought another great English leader to face another mortal threat. Winston Churchill seized on the radio as the instrument of opportunity to marshal England against the Nazis. Most people believe that it was his words of courage, challenge, and defiance that spelled the difference between victory and defeat. Even after the war, Churchill continued to make history with his words. Recognizing a new menace from the East in the incarnation of Stalinist communism, Churchill warned against aggressive expansionism.

"The awful ruin of Europe," Churchill growled, lamenting the carnage of World War II, "with all its varnished glories, and of large parts of Asia, glares us in the eyes. When designs of wicked men or the aggressive urge of mighty states dissolve . . . humble folk are confronted with difficulties with which they cannot cope. For them, all is distorted, all is broken or is even ground to pulp."

Then, signaling an alarm about a new power, rising out of the Soviet Union, he said: "From Stettin in the Baltic to Trieste in the Adriatic, an iron curtain has descended across the Continent. Behind that line lie all the capitals of the ancient states of Central and Eastern Europe. . . ."

A new world order ensued. Churchill called it the Cold War. And for the next forty years the Soviet Union and the West—namely the United States—were engaged in a sometimes tense nuclear staredown. In the end, the Soviet Union blinked, then collapsed. (Churchill coined many other sterling phrases, including "summit conference.")

So Churchill arguably not only saved Western civilization by throwing words of defiance in the face of the enemy and words of encouragement and inspiration to his own people, he also anticipated the free world's opposition to Communist totalitarianism.

Churchill's oratorical gifts both during and after World War II gave new meaning to the term "words of leadership" and helped define a level of CVA that is still revered today.

If Churchill could change the world, is it possible that you might be able to change your business or enhance your career? If you have something to say, something worth listening to, you can influence the people around you.

Opening amenities are opening inanities.

For example, Churchill always preached that opening amenities in public speaking ("Good morning. It is a pleasure to be here today. . . .") contribute nothing. He always believed in starting strongly with a powerful statement, a personal story, or an anecdote to make a point. Churchill also maintained that one point per speech is enough—not two or three—and that it is important always to take a position. Once he decided what he wanted to say, Churchill provided vivid examples to back up his position and make his speech come alive. Churchill always took pains to use simple, hard-hitting Anglo-Saxon language ("blood, toil, tears, and sweat"). And when he finished, Churchill liked to drive his message home with a rousing ending.

This is Churchillian CVA you can borrow from the master to make your own presentations more powerful.

Another powerful speaker was Teddy Roosevelt, the twenty-sixth president of the United States, who at the end of the nineteenth century saw complacency threatening to erode the vital core of the "can do" American character. Roosevelt's entire life can be summed up in one word: action—and plenty of it. In his whirlwind sixty years, Roosevelt exploded out of a sickly childhood to become a governor, president, author, explorer, speaker, and adventurer—and all his life he preached what he lived.

In action he saw redemption; in inaction, inevitable decay.

"Our country calls not for the life of ease, but for the life of strenuous endeavor!" he bellowed from the "bully pulpit," his fist pounding the air. "For it is only through strife, through hard and dangerous endeavor, that we shall ultimately win the goal of true national greatness."

Strenuous endeavor? Strife? Americans raised on Disney World, Dunkin' Donuts, and disposable diapers might puzzle at this clarion wake-up call to action.

A hundred years ago T.R. warned: "The twentieth century looms before us. . . . If we stand idly by . . . if we seek merely swollen, slothful ease and ignoble peace, if we shrink from the hard contests where men must win at hazard of their lives and at the risk of all they hold dear . . . then the bolder and stronger peoples will pass us by and win for themselves the domination of the world. . . ."

This is the voice of a young, robust, opportunistic, and adventurous country just beginning to flex its adolescent muscles in the mature years of colonialism just before World War I. It is the voice of the frontier, of the individual, of the Wild West, Manifest Destiny, and a belief in the potential of the new land and its people.

A century later, many Americans are overweight and undereducated, but we fondly remember Teddy Roosevelt for his blustery bravado, and still secretly like to think of ourselves as Rough Riders. Roosevelt's words articulated an image of self-determination and an assertive worldview that fashion our foreign policy to this day. Think of Grenada, the Dominican Republic, Somalia, Desert Storm, Bosnia.

If Roosevelt could influence foreign policy seven decades after his death, can businesspeople fashion the direction of their own companies today? It is not simply the strategic plan that makes things happen. It is also an articulate man or woman behind the plan that makes the difference. The articulate visionary catapults the strategic plan into action; the results are higher productivity and increased revenues.

That's CVA.

You can see the process of change and growth through leadership unfolding throughout history, notably in the American Revolution. The American Revolution might never have happened had not history provided, at that precise moment, an array of fiercely motivated, inspired citizens who fanned the flames of rebellion with oratory that called men to arms and united a fledging nation under a single flag and against a common enemy.

In 1775, Patrick Henry rose to speak in a church filled with colonial delegates. He burned with revolutionary zeal. An eyewitness, a Baptist minister sitting in the audience, later recalled that "Henry's voice rose louder and louder, until the walls of the building and all within them seemed to shake and rock in its tremendous vibration. . . . Men leaned forward, their faces pale and their eyes glaring like the speaker's. . . . When he sat down, I felt sick with excitement."

Henry warned his fellow colonists to beware of treacherous appearances of conciliation from the British Crown.

"Suffer yourselves not to be betrayed by a kiss!" he roared. "Are fleets and armies necessary to a work of love and reconciliation? Have we showed ourselves so unwilling to be reconciled that force must be called in to win back our love? . . .

"Is life so dear, or peace so sweet, as to be purchased at the price of chains and slavery? Forbid it, Almighty God! I know not what course others may take; but as for me, give me liberty, or give me death!"

He spoke entirely without notes, this thirty-eight-year-old self-taught lawyer, and by the time he was finished, the course of the American colonies was decided. The delegates went on to draft the Declaration of Independence, and the rest, as they say, is history. American history.

Henry's words are an example of first-rate early American CVA.

I'm not suggesting that you should be like Patrick Henry every time you make a business speech or presentation. But there are certain characteristics that your presentation should have in common with Henry's. Namely, you should:

- understand the issues;

- take a point of view;

- believe in what you are saying;

- speak with absolute conviction;

- appeal to the gut and the heart as well as to the mind.

Abraham Lincoln was America's most eloquent president. Lincoln presided over the saddest chapter of American history, the Civil War—though he died just five days after its conclusion.

The great issue of the day, and arguably the heart of the conflict between North and South, was slavery. Right up until his death in 1865, Lincoln was haunted by a morbid conviction that the war itself was a kind of divine retribution for slavery. In his second inaugural address, on March 4, 1865, he postulated that "perhaps God gives to both North and South this terrible war as the price for slavery." But the tides of war had begun to favor the North, and Lincoln was already able to perceive an end to the carnage. Deeply desirous of bringing the fractured nation back together in a spirit of forgiveness, Lincoln wrapped up his speech in this way:

"Fondly we do hope, fervently we do pray, that this mighty scourge of war may speedily pass away . . ." he said, his words like a poem, almost like music.

". . . With malice toward none, with charity for all, with firmness in the right as God gives us to see the right, let us strive on to finish the work we are in . . . to bind up the nation's wounds, to care for him who shall have borne the battle and for his widow and his orphan, to do all which may achieve and cherish a just and lasting peace among ourselves and with all nations."

No one listening to Lincoln's words could help but see the gentle poet inside the reluctant warrior. One might measure Lincoln's CVA by both the wisdom and beauty of his words.

Lincoln was a deeply complex man who suffered agonizing bouts of self-doubt and mind-numbing descents into depression. According to his wife, Mary Todd, he sought solace in meditation and prayer, asking for guidance and strength—living his life at the center of attention, yet ironically always feeling terribly alone. People today, jaded and enured by generations of bitter experience with both the legal profession and politicians, might find it hard to believe that Lincoln (both a lawyer and a politician) was genuinely driven by a desire to do the decent and moral thing.

Great words from great people shape history. In the end, your words will also shape you—in life as in business. Your words will carve your character, make you friends, win you new business, and constantly change the course of your life.

CHAPTER
FIVE

Missed Potential

I read somewhere that nine of ten people never fulfill their potential. This does not mean that they don't try. Millions of people work hard all their lives—only to discover that in the end they feel unfulfilled and can't afford to retire. Just when they should be reaping the many rewards of a life well spent, they find their golden years slipping maddeningly out of reach like the fabled pot of gold at the end of a vanishing rainbow. This unwelcome discovery has long been a fact of life, but it seems even more poignantly true at the beginning of the Age of Knowledge—in a society of too many people seeking too few good jobs, and when traditional social cornerstones such as education, religion, family, and the environment are threatening to come apart.

Sometimes the reasons for a failure to achieve potential and an absence of personal fulfillment seem obvious.

For example, a friend of mine was a brilliantly talented

pianist—a prodigy—as a child. By age eight he'd been offered a Juilliard tutorial and been asked to perform in concert. But when his banker father discovered the boy was really serious about music and might even make it his life's work, the father refused to allow his son to attend Juilliard. And later, as a teenager, after his son revealed that he still wanted to devote his life to music, the father threatened to disinherit him. The family's sense of self-worth and values were founded on money and status, so the boy capitulated and went on after college to become a mediocre stockbroker. It was the greatest regret of his life—and today, forty years later and suffering from cancer, he curses himself for allowing his father to crush the only real dream he ever had.

Another acquaintance, born into a family of almost unimaginable wealth, exhibited unusual charm, wit, and brains early on. He was masterful at chess, a ranked tennis player, as handsome as a movie star, popular in school, and able to complete the Sunday *New York Times* in a half hour. He got A's and B's in both school and college almost without having even to open a book, hung out with the sons of the rich and powerful, and was probably, on the face of it, the most likely to succeed and the least likely to fail of all the people I ever knew.

Yet he never bothered to take a job, pursue an interest, or enjoy the beauty or natural riches of the world around him. It never occurred to him to use his inherited millions to help other people. For all his great gifts and advantages, he ultimately turned to the bottle for companionship and wound up dead of cirrhosis of the liver before age thirty. On his deathbed, when he knew his life was slipping away, he begged for a second chance and vowed to be a different man. But it was too little, too late.

I have seen less Dionysian variations of that tragic theme dozens of times, which only reinforce the notion that life without struggle—call it challenge—is no life at all.

In my own case, I abandoned a promising art career to marry and raise a family. Today I'll never know how far I might have gone in that direction.

But these are the easy calls. The tougher calls come when people appear to do all the right things and *still* wind up bitterly disappointed.

Take the case of George Wendl. Two days after his fifty-third birthday and two years shy of his pension, his new, forty-two-year-old hotshot boss called George into his office and told him that budget constrictions, downsizing, and the new "realities of the marketplace" (translation: Who needs you?) would mean that George had become, to use the boss's term, "redundant."

"Frankly, we can no longer afford the luxury of an associate publisher," the boss said. "I'm sorry, George, but we're going to have to let you go."

The corporate killers were coming. Three million white-collar workers thrown out of their jobs in just three years. Now George knew it was his turn.

Fifteen years with the company. Twenty years in publishing. George had made a name for himself in the business. He was well liked, respected, admired for his integrity. *Redundant.*

He'd been a football All-American, served with distinction as a Marine captain in Vietnam, where he'd won several medals, been seriously wounded, three times nearly killed—once when an NVA rocket in Hue blew him thirty feet straight up. He still had the hideous scars and had only rarely been able to make it through airport metal detectors without setting off alarms.

Then the psychic pain, all the loathing and hostility he faced after the war from his own people. The woman hissing like a viper and spitting on his uniform. The cold-sweat, heart-pounding nightmares. The flashbacks. The time he went to hear the "Overture" to *The War of 1812* in Central Park, he snapped when the fireworks started.

Then later the leukemia, which he had been able to manage well enough to continue to lead a normal life. But there was never any doubt in his mind, or in the minds of his doctors, that the cause of his sickness was Agent Orange and the defoliation campaign in Vietnam. (He remembered when the bombers unloaded the stuff more than once right on top of his position.)

The wife. The kids—both now in colleges and racking up an annual cost before taxes of some $60,000. Now his $275,000 per annum salary was ending. What was he going to do?

George had never sued anyone for anything in his life. But a lawyer friend suggested he had a good case for age discrimination. Everybody wanted new blood. They wanted the older guys out and the younger guys in—even if it meant having to shoot some of those older guys before they could collect the pension they'd been planning and counting on their entire working lives. And even though shooting the older guys often meant throwing out priceless talent and experience.

The suit was a possibility. But in the meantime George was out on the street for the first time in years, not a particularly attractive commodity, trying to choke back his anger as he started the disheartening process of interviewing with—and being rejected by—people half his age.

It was demeaning to sit in supplication, struggling just to appear normal, trying not to reveal the frustration and fear tearing him up inside. He figured he had maybe five or six months before he'd have to sell the house and take the kids out of college.

After a month of polite but gut-wrenching rejections ("you're overqualified for the job, I'm afraid, Mr. Wendl"), he began to think seriously about the only other option: working for himself.

And that's when I met George. A mutual friend had suggested that we get together with the thought that maybe I might be able to offer some advice.

The first thing I noticed about George was that his handshake was limp. The second thing I noticed was that he avoided looking me in the eye when he spoke. Maybe he was just shy. But you got the impression he wasn't interested in you. Sometimes it was tough to hear what he was saying. He came across as a mumbler. It took him forever to get to his point. All in all, if you didn't know George, you'd come away with the impression that he really didn't have a very high regard for himself.

George was amazed to discover these things about

himself. I asked him to reinact what he considered to be the best business presentations he'd ever made—and after he saw the results on videotape and we talked about how to make them better, he was even more amazed. But he swallowed his pride, accepted his shortcomings, and took my advice.

Not to put too short a spin on it, we made quite a few things better with George—even buying him a new suit. With practice, he became a changed man. He came alive, and he regained his lost confidence. He began looking everybody in the eye. His handshake became firm and enthusiastic. He was full of a new energy—so much so that attractive offers started to come in. But he spotted a niche market and decided to plunge into that new enterprise with the knowledge that if it worked, he'd get to keep all the marbles himself. Maybe a lot of marbles. At last word, the new adventure is beginning to pay off.

My point is that there *can* be a happy ending—even for people like George who worry themselves sick when things don't work out exactly as planned. George had a coach. It would be nice if each of us had a personal "trainer" to open our eyes and help us along our way. But each of us has the power within to restore and heal *ourselves* even when life is trying to tell us the game is over.

Sometimes we're talking about a quick fix, sometimes not. But this much we know for certain: Our relationships with ourselves dictate our relationships with others. And the interactions with other people and how they perceive us ultimately determine our success.

Rarely is the dichotomy of reality versus potential

more eloquently revealed than in the unforgiving arena of American politics.

An election-year State of the Union address is no small thing, and Bill Clinton rose to the occasion admirably in his velvet-smooth January 1996 television address to the nation, which saw his poll ratings soar. Clinton was warm, relaxed, confident, clearly enjoying himself. He was by turns statesmanlike, caring, amiable, intense, focused—a leader very much in control.

The fact that I can't remember a lot of what he said says a lot for the concept that real CVA has as much, perhaps more, to do with presentation than it does with content. But what most people came away with was the clear impression that Clinton had moved to the right and virtually preempted the entire Republican platform.

By contrast, Bob Dole, the Republican front-runner who responded for the opposition after the president's live broadcast, came across as dour and chilly. Dole seemed pained, weary, and distracted. His eyes were dead, his delivery uncomfortable—as if he recognized early on what he was up against and just wanted to put this disagreeable part of his job behind him.

The result: Clinton's stock went up and Dole's went down, creating a wide gap. Even Dole's colleagues were peeved. One fellow senator said Dole looked and sounded "like an undertaker having a bad day."

Dole himself did not take kindly to the carping commentary from all sides, and blamed his poor performance on the unfriendly stagecraft of the occasion.

"I was there in an empty office with a bunch of hot

lights and eight guys [the camera crew]," he complained. "Clinton had a live audience and a lot of nice feedback in applause."

Dole had a point. Working at night with hot lights in a bleak office virtually alone on the heels of a banner presidential performance is daunting. But you could argue that Dole's thirty-five years of public life and thousands of tough speeches in any number of challenging circumstances should have given him enough mustard to at least match the president. In fact, you could argue that if anyone could do it, Bob Dole could do it. He'd been there.

But he didn't.

You could say that Dole failed to meet his potential at the very moment he needed it most.

Weeks later, in New Hampshire, another Republican contender, Lamar Alexander of Tennessee, slipped not on a banana but on a grocery list. Lamar, attempting to position himself as a man of the people, was challenged by a reporter to correctly answer how much a gallon of milk and a dozen eggs cost. Looking baffled, the senator turned to an aide and snapped, "I need to know the price of a gallon of milk and a dozen eggs—and I need it *now!*"

The answer was never forthcoming from aide nor senator, and Lamar's foes in the primary race gleefully announced that Lamar had failed the grocery test.

As the senator discovered—probably not for the first time—it is sometimes the littlest things of life that bring us down.

Lesson in life: If you want to be elected as a common

man by the common man, know what the common man eats and how much it costs.

Second lesson in life: If you must treat the help badly, don't do it in public.

Back in Washington, the freshman class of Republicans wasn't faring much better. Mark Souder (R., Indiana) ticked off both sides of the aisle by saying that cult leader David Koresh violated the law only by having sex "with consenting minors . . . do you send tanks and government troops into large sections of Kentucky and Tennessee and other places where such things occur?" Tennessee and Kentucky loved that.

Then there's Frank Creamons (R., Ohio), who said he was against premarital sex because "marriage is a very sanctimonious commitment." Earlier, he theorized that the Roman Empire might have collapsed because of AIDS. The point here is that while we may be competent and we may be smart, in the end it is our words that define us. Leaders rise and fall, but their words live on.

Lesson in life: People judge us by our words, our vocabulary, our command of the language. What we say—or don't say—can determine how high and how far we go.

Can our CVA mean the difference between potential lost and potential found?

Can CVA be the key to unlocking the potential for leadership inside each of us?

> **To achieve 100 percent eye contact, don't speak until you see the whites of their eyes.**

CHAPTER
SIX

Missing the Home Run

One of the greatest missed opportunities of all time occurred when Xerox failed to recognize the huge promise of the personal computer—then watched helpless and red-faced as the fruits of its own considerable research propelled others to heights that Xerox would never see.

This historic whiff happened in the late 1960s and early 1970s, when assorted geniuses at Xerox's renowned Palo Alto research and development labs created prototypes of the first personal computers and had even begun to set up a working model of the Internet.

Both world-beating breakthroughs were years ahead of their time. And had Xerox not missed the ball at a critical moment in time, the world might have been theirs—and theirs alone.

Xerox lost its way not because of any lack of willingness to invest in the future. The Xerox labs were, and still are, world-class research centers on the cutting edge of technology.

Nor was there a problem with people, productivity, or profitability. At the time, Xerox had a virtual lock on the world market for copiers.

The answer to why Xerox never realized its opportunity to lead the greatest technical revolution of the twentieth century comes down to just one word: communication.

Try as they might, the frustrated geniuses in Palo Alto failed to convince Xerox senior management back East that they were on to something big. The engineers and research people tried repeatedly to define not only the significance of what was happening but also its vast commercial potential.

Management listened politely. But the Xerox bosses were sitting on top of a great business that dominated the world, and they did not comprehend the monumental import of what their people were trying to tell them.

Somehow, incredibly, no one got the message, and the great opportunity passed Xerox by.

But the opportunity did not pass everybody by. Nor did it go away. An alert young man by the name of Steven Jobs heard about the strange doings at the Palo Alto labs and stopped by to see what was going on. Researchers showed him their work, and Jobs knew right away he was staring at the future.

Jobs went back to tinkering in his garage, took a swing at the ball Xerox had thrown his way—and connected. It wasn't long before Apple Computers was born.

Another young man, Bill Gates, heard about the fun things going on at Palo Alto and he, too, decided to investigate.

Gates knew a winner when he saw one, and lost no time incorporating some of the Xerox cutting-edge concepts into his own work.

Both Jobs and Gates recognized the "user-friendly" aspects of the Xerox approach, which they knew was going to be the key to the commercial success of the computer revolution.

Today it is fair to say that Microsoft, Apple, and others owe at least some of their success to Xerox, which today is *not* a computer company.

And therein lies a very large lesson in life. What does it profit us to be brilliant if even our own people can't seem to hear what we're trying to tell them? And what does it profit us to be running a world-class company if we can't seem to get the critical message of our own future from our own people?

The disconnect that occurred at Xerox is symptomatic of communications problems that persist to this day in organizations and businesses all over the world.

In the case of Xerox, it is likely that the well-intended engineers simply did not understand how to explain the urgency of their message to Xerox management. It is probable that, in the way of competent technical people everywhere, they simply expected the data to speak for themselves. They believed that the reams of technical and research information were self-evident. They never recognized the need to *translate* all those data into a form comprehensible to management, to sufficiently explain what all that information meant.

The three thousand miles that separated the two sides were only part of the communications problem. It is easy to imagine a clash of cultures: engineer vs. button-down exec; California dreamer-*cum*-technogeek vs. East Coast technoilliterate; laid back vs. rigid, and so on.

So it is not difficult to grasp the considerable challenge these two sides of the same company—both essential to the company's future—faced trying to make sense to one another.

We may never know exactly what went wrong, but we do know that what was going on in the heads of the Palo Alto whiz kids somehow did not get into the heads of the suits back in Stamford, Connecticut.

Analysis a quarter century after the fact is mostly conjecture, but I would suggest that the burden of failed communication rested not with the suits but with the whiz kids.

Looking back, you could say that the whiz kids failed to:

- understand the message sufficiently to convey their conviction and sense of urgency;

- properly articulate their case to management;

- bridge the cultural and psychological gaps between Palo Alto and Stamford, between techie and suit.

History would have turned out differently if the Palo Alto people had convinced the home office how important their ground-breaking research really was. If they had:

- forged a crystal-clear message (the future of Xerox depends not on copying equipment but on computers and software);

- gotten management's attention by "front-loading" their presentations with the message;

- backed up that message with concrete examples to provide proof of the urgency of their proposition;

- talked not like scientists and engineers but like missionaries converting heathens;

- given management a strong "takeaway"—a strong ending—that they would remember.

One can only wonder if, beyond Xerox, there have been other voices in the wilderness that went unheard for various reasons: mavericks, for example, at GM, Ford, and Chrysler who may have tried to alert their managements to the coming threat from Japanese automakers. Or forgotten voices at IBM who may have attempted to convince the corporate office that IBM should begin thinking a little more about PCs and a little less about mainframes.

Sometimes it is the voice within, the prophet in our house, who can sound the alarm and save us from ourselves.

Singing the Big Blues
No More

One man, arguably, dragged IBM back from decline and once again into the running as the world's foremost computer company. Lou Gerstner defied the odds, squelched the critics and cynics, and revealed two age-old truths:

1 If you want to make sure something gets done right, you'd better do it yourself; and . . .

2 One personal visit is worth a week working the phones; and one phone call is worth a ton of paper and junk mail.

No mirrors, no tricks, no sleight-of-hand. Just Gerstner making sure that the big deals get done and the big customers stay happy.

Notice that we're not talking about fancy technology, slick marketing, or cutthroat pricing. These elements are real and they all play a part. What we're talking about is nothing more complicated than meeting face to face with customers, listening to their needs, and figuring out how to satisfy those needs.

This is a mantra you're likely to hear from one end of the country to the other. Everybody's for it, nobody's really against it, and just about everybody sings the same song.

But the difference between Gerstner and almost everybody else is that Gerstner is not only a true believer, but actually walks the walk and talks the talk. In other words, he walks out of the office, gets on a plane, meets with customers, and makes it happen.

And he knows better than anyone else at IBM that the only way, really, for IBM to rebound to the front of the field is for a man of vision and deep understanding to take personal ownership of the mission. More than that, he expects everybody else to be as enthusiastic an ambassador as he is. But because he is a man of the world, he also knows that no one can deliver the goods like the CEO himself.

And that's why Lou Gerstner is one of the great business leaders of his time.

"I came here with a view that you start the day with customers, that you start thinking about a company around its customers, and you organize around customers," Gerstner told a reporter.

Gerstner knew that companies everywhere, big and small, are staggered by the rushing waters of information technology rising rapidly all around them in one crashing wave after another.

How to stay on top of this force?

How to anticipate all the things that will need fixing—before they begin to break down?

How to stay ahead of a game in which the rules change—sometimes radically—almost every week?

How to avoid ghastly errors and mortal mistakes?

Who you gonna call?

You call IBM, of course—if Lou Gerstner has anything to say about it. And Lord knows, he's got a lot to say.

For example, take a recent typical day as reported by *Business Week*: Gerstner lifts off in the IBM Gulf Stream IV from Westchester County Airport shortly after dawn on a dreary fall morning. He's bound for Toronto—with no entourage—to meet with twenty North American CEOs and business leaders in a hotel conference room, where Gerstner whips off his jacket and holds forth for ninety spellbinding minutes. No slides. No canned presentation. And no mind-numbing discourse on technology. Instead, he launches into a high-level rap session that touches on everything from the quality of public schools to the changes technology is bringing to financial-services companies.

It's a fun, productive meeting. The audience walks away with the impression that Gerstner—and IBM—are ahead of the curve and on top of the flow. They have a good feeling about Gerstner, believing that he may have the answers to some of their problems. He helps them see their own needs and makes the arcane clear.

"He acts as a translator to his clients," explains Wolfgang Schmidt, chairman and CEO of Rubbermaid. "He's able to connect."

But more than that, Lou Gerstner is selling *trust*. He's Mr. Fixit, the good guy, the partner, the friend, the consultant, the confidant, the ally who can take your worries and your problems and make them go away.

This is CVA at full gallop and the finest kind of business likability.

Procter & Gamble chairman and CEO John Pepper bumped into Gerstner at a business function and mentioned that P&G was wrestling with how better to exploit new technology such as the Internet to streamline operations, speed innovation, and reach customers in new ways.

Within days, Gerstner himself and some of his top people were huddling with Pepper and other senior P&G managers. The P&G officers were impressed. It was the first time an IBM CEO had visited in decades—in spite of the fact that P&G is one of IBM's best accounts.

When Ameritech, a Baby Bell, was looking to farm out its processing operations, Gerstner was there, too. A lot of companies bid for the job, but "Lou was the only CEO who was deeply involved," according to CEO Richard Notebaert. Gerstner's involvement paid off. IBM won the business.

Gerstner wins the business by being genuinely helpful,

by giving the impression that he really cares about other people, their problems, and their companies.

"IBM is helping us find solutions—whether with their hardware or with someone else's," notes Robert Miller, chairman and CEO of retailer Fred Meyer, Inc.

The human capital Gerstner brings to the party every time he walks into another CEO's office, gets on the horn, buttonholes business leaders at off-campus functions, or schmoozes on the links may well be worth more—and have more clout—than all the marketing, promotion, and sales money IBM expends in an entire year. And he's so engaging and persuasive that once the dialogue gets rolling, it's tough to stop. Piece by piece he builds the foundations for working relationships that could last a lifetime—or longer.

Importantly, he is willing to sacrifice today's hardware and software sales in the knowledge that he's positioning IBM to be the partner of choice for tomorrow. He's looking to establish significant long-term relationships that will flourish way after his tenure as CEO.

In the meantime, the beat goes on. On any given week you might find Gerstner in Europe, Latin America, Asia, or crisscrossing the United States spreading the good word and leaving everyone who's willing to listen with the impression that Lou Gerstner and IBM might just be their answer to some of the tougher business challenges of the twenty-first century.

The 50 Percent Solution

I have said that we are living in a world populated with intelligent, competent people who may never realize their potential or their dreams. One reason is because they are incapable of speaking up or unwilling to speak up so they can be heard. Great minds and great talent go begging because people don't know how to connect their minds with their mouths. Fertile landscapes are left fallow and we, collectively, are the worse for it.

Business schools bemoan the fact that their students are quantitatively savvy but unable to express themselves. Corporations complain that some of their smartest people are ineffective in meetings and presentations, and lacking the communication skills to meet with customers.

This lamentable paradox is what I call "the 50 percent problem"—50 percent because the most capable among us are doomed to careers in which their communication shortcomings limit them to reaching only half their potential. This is not unlike the glass ceiling phenomenon, in which women and minorities are alleged to hit an invisible "glass ceiling" within organizations, beyond which they are not permitted to advance.

But every problem has an answer. The answer to "the 50 percent problem" is "the 50 percent solution." Scientists have said that we use just 10 percent of our brainpower and that we have yet to figure out how to tap into the other 90 percent. Using a previously unmined nine-tenths of our brains would no doubt give new meaning to the concept of fulfilling one's potential.

But suppose we were merely to double our potential—an objective I am convinced is within the reach of each of us, no matter who we are and no matter what we do.

In fact, I have seen people bust out of their 50 percent ceiling hundreds of times. Most need only direction and encouragement to bring out all the percolating potential bubbling just below the surface.

Some people don't need even that.

For example, Barbara Walters started her career as an NBC secretary in the early 1960s and rose to become one of the best-paid people in on-air network television—in spite of a conspicuous lisp.

Beside sheer chutzpah, Barbara exhibited unflagging confidence in her abilities and never seemed to doubt that she would eventually wind up on top of her profession.

Psychologists might suggest that we become what we believe, that our dreams or expectations can coalesce into reality, that we create our own lives. Given the right circumstances, that assumption is probably true. But the instrument that shapes the reality is that strange mix of elements we call personality. What is personality? Why do some people have it, while others don't? Can we shape it? Can we learn it?

The answer to the last two questions is yes. Anyone over twenty-one knows that all of life is a constant learning process that refines and defines our personalities—the face we show the world. The fact that the bright self we show others often masks fear, insecurity, and confusion is not important. We learn through constant reinforcement to present a reality that is not always the truth—and that's all right. That's human nature. In time the reality we present may become the truth.

Most of this is learned behavior, and by the time we're halfway through our lives, most of us are pretty good at putting on a good face. But to be adept, we've first got to let a reluctant little genie out of a bottle: We've got to unleash our powers of communication. We've got to be able to approach other people and affect their lives—simply by the way we speak. How we communicate is the centerpiece of our personalities, giving life, color, and texture to every relationship we enter into.

Theoretically each of us should be getting better at this skill throughout our lives. The passing chat with the cabbie. The pleasantries with the neighbor. The good talk over a good meal. The laughs with friends. The breezy banter at a cocktail party. All these small things build, grain by grain, the sand castles of our lives, and each is a valid experience to help us know ourselves, make friends, and influence others.

Barbara Walters talked her way to the top. She put her brains and her mouth together and came up a winner. Early on she understood the process and made it her life's work to refine that process—articulating every day who she was and who she wanted to be. Without even knowing it, Barbara found CVA.

But how many other thousands of Barbara Walters did not seize the opportunity, did not see the possibilities, did not recognize their potential locked away in that bottle?

This learned behavior we acquire in two ways: First, we learn by life experience, by instinct and intuition. Second, we learn from instructors who have something useful to teach us.

An executive assistant at one of my corporate clients got the assignment to manage my speaker and leadership training program—and wound up soon after a vice president. This woman was smart and was bound for bigger and better things. But she seized on an unexpected opportunity to catapult herself ahead—not unlike Barbara Walters.

Recognizing the new assignment of managing my program as an opportunity rather than another chore piled on top of an already overloaded work schedule, she took advantage of last-minute changes in the schedule to slot *herself* in when more senior replacements were not available. Over the course of half a year she managed to have four one-on-one sessions with me—in effect receiving the training that had been reserved exclusively for senior corporate officers.

At the same time, she took advantage of her access to

the senior players through her role as scheduler and program manager to cement important relationships.

She learned quickly from her sessions with me how to present herself more impressively, to think faster on her feet, to marshal her thoughts to better effect, and always to leave people with something interesting to think and talk about. She saw every conversation, every chance encounter as an opportunity to practice her skills and advance her objectives.

It wasn't long before she found herself with more responsibility. And not long after that, she had an assistant. And not long after that, she was transferred to a more important job. Soon she was leading a special project team, then another, and before a year was out she found herself suddenly named to a brand-new position: vice president of corporate public affairs. As of this writing, she manages a $20 million budget and a staff of more than a hundred people.

Stephen Hawking, the renowned British astrophysicist and nuclear physicist, soared to the top of his profession on a mind trapped inside a body devastated by Lou Gehrig's disease. And even when the disease took away his power of speech, withered his body, and confined him to a motorized wheelchair, Hawking continued to communicate with the world through a computer especially designed to allow him to peck one letter at a time through the movement of his eyes. Said to be the greatest mind since Einstein, Hawking speaks to audiences through a specially trained translator and even published a bestselling book, *A Brief History of Time.*

Life presented overwhelming obstacles, but Hawking let nothing stand in the way of his profound need to share the fruits of his amazing mind. Every day in Hawking's life the genie inside the genius is demanding to be let out.

All three of these diverse characters had the potential to go far, and each recognized that potential—then capitalized on it. Each in effect talked his or her way to the top. In other words, each did what most of us fail to do— make the most of what we are with what we've got. And the way you do that is to achieve confidence not only in yourself but also in your command of the language. Articulate people are not always successful, but they are far more likely to be successful than people who are not articulate. A facile person lacking wisdom or knowledge can be a charlatan or huckster. But a wise or knowledgeable person—a scientist or an engineer, for example—who is not facile with language often winds up, sadly, overlooked or forgotten.

A modest investment of time and money can produce surprising results.

The good news is that time and again I have witnessed a modest investment of time and money produce stunning results. The incoherent presentation suddenly is made clear and memorable; the reluctant mumbler is transformed into a forceful speaker; the uncertain introvert becomes a charismatic, warmly accessible extrovert; the secretary blooms into the executive. Once people start marshaling their minds and then connecting their brains to their mouths, the trend is up—and the ceilings are shattered.

Take the case of Bill Gates, who saw the future coming, as far back as the early 1970s, and embraced it with both arms. More than any visionary in recent memory, he shaped our lives and our times, helping launch the world with digitized speed into the vast expanse of the twenty-first century.

Yet Gates could have slipped into the crowded, anonymous limbo of historic might-have-beens. He was a thinker (his mother said that as a boy he used to spend an inordinate amount of time sequestered alone in his room "just thinking"). He was undeniably brilliant. He had some great ideas. He had a vision. But Harvard, Stanford, UCLA, and Princeton have produced a lot of very bright people who fit those prerequisites. Yet Bill Gates, who for all the world looked and acted like just another egghead technogeek, brought something else to the party, something essential.

Bill Gates was not only a brain but also someone who understood intuitively how to translate ideas into information that people could not only understand but also use. Bill Gates turned out to be nothing like the shy, reclusive, uncommunicative genius you might expect. Bill Gates, to the amazement of a lot of people, turned out to be a regular sort of guy with a good sense of humor (unless, some say, that humor has to do with himself).

Bill Gates not only had tons of good ideas but also took pleasure in expressing those ideas to anyone willing to listen. He was articulate, witty, very focused, very clear. And he had a lot to say—not only about his particular discipline but also about marketing, productivity, profitability, research and development, and strategic planning. It turned out that Bill Gates knew a lot about a lot of things, and the more he talked, the more people listened. Soon he had his own company with a small cadre of fanatically loyal employees, many of whom were among the best in the software industry. Before long, Microsoft started doubling, then tripling in size, and then he had lots of investors to talk to, and then he was on the cover of national magazines and one of the richest people in the world. Any given week you can open a newspaper or business publication and find another interview with Bill Gates, waxing eloquently and forcefully on anything from chip technology to ice cream.

Connect your brain to your mouth and good things will begin to happen.

If Bill Gates had not connected his brain to his mouth and allowed all that potential to manifest itself, if he had hidden himself from the world and just designed brilliant software for the rest of his life, there wouldn't be a Microsoft. And the United States would not dominate in a market that will figure large in the twenty-first century.

What does it profit us to be brilliant—perhaps even the best in our businesses—if no one hears what we say and therefore never knows what we offer?

One of the two times I met Bill Gates and heard him speak—the year he received the CEO of the year award in New York—he confounded my expectations. He was comfortable, conversational, and frequently very funny at the podium. What he had to say was not only anecdotal and therefore easy to listen to but also made a lot of sense. He won over an important audience that night—and in so doing also gained new friends and allies.

By contrast, you will not see many people from Gates's introverted industry coming forward—staying visible, tackling issues before they become problems, keeping the dialogue rolling, year after year. Gates had everything to gain and little to lose by stepping up to the plate.

Gates embodies a graduate course in advanced CVA—and so can you. If you start now.

The Romans summed up the parameters of potential nicely with four words:

Tempus fugit
(Time flies)
and . . .
Carpe diem
(Seize the day)

To those who believe in their own potential, who are willing to stretch, like Bill Gates; to those who know something is missing in their professional lives but aren't quite sure what that something is; to those who value greater productivity on the job and greater profitability, and greater personal and professional rewards, I suggest they forge ahead, looking for opportunities to exercise their CVA.

If you happen to be in business, I might also suggest: *Tempus fugit. . . . Carpe diem.*

CHAPTER
NINE

How to Connect with Your Audience

When Pope John Paul II talks to his flock it's hard to imagine what's going through his mind as he bends over his prepared text, murmurs the words down toward his shoes, and reads every word on the page without bothering to look up at his audience.

We know from his book *Crossing the Threshold of Hope* that the pontiff is a leader with passionate opinions about the society we live in and the direction the Church should follow. But it appears that he may be missing an opportunity to cement his position and galvanize Catholics—especially young Catholics—to what he perceives to be the greater good.

The reason the pope can get away with this is because he *is* the pope. Part of his charm is his perceived aura of innocence and lack of guile. So millions of people forgive John Paul for his apparent indifference and awkwardness in the pulpit.

But the rest of us are not the pope; and if a business-person were to emulate the pope's style in a new business presentation, say, or a senior management presentation, he or she would miss the mark.

So while the pope is by all accounts the right man in the right job, he could use a little CVA.

What is at stake are big issues: life, death, abortion, contraception. We're talking here about the relationship between God and man, good and evil, love and hate. About the teachings of Christ at the beginning of the third millennium. About angels and miracles and the Prince of Darkness.

This is epic stuff of the ages, come down to us through the stained-glass corridors of time and the Church, through two thousand years of splendor and pageantry unmatched in history.

Businesspeople have a different story to tell. So do people who speak at clubs, civic organizations, churches, and charity events. Every day thousands of people in many different venues present themselves to audiences. Most of these people are worthy, admirable, and earnest. Some of them are on a mission and feel passionately about their subjects. But most of them, in my experience, send out the wrong signals—signals that, ironically, contradict the very messages they are hoping to convey.

Like the pope, many of them read prepared scripts and never get their faces out of the text.

They motor along mindlessly, sometimes breathlessly, trying to wrap it up as quickly as possible—and thereby alienate their audiences.

They read not knowing the meaning of the words they are reading.

They don't pause for emphasis.

They speak too fast.

Some stand in the dark and read word slides off the screen.

Others put up slides so complex you'd need instructions just to decipher them—then race through the slides so fast no one has a clue what he or she has seen. Or heard.

And so it goes. Every day. All over the world. A thousand times in a thousand different places.

What's wrong here?

The same thing that's wrong with the world. As the chain gang boss said after he thumped Paul Newman to the ground in *Cool Hand Luke:* "What we have here is a failure to communicate."

We all fail to communicate at different times and in different ways. But often the solution to good communication is simply looking people in the eye. Easy to do— but frequently we don't. That's why you've got to be alert to the three "zones":

1 The NO ZONE: eyes down while talking.

2 The OZONE: eyes too high—looking over the audience's head.

3 The GO ZONE: eye contact; this is where you want to be 95 percent of the time.

SPEAK ONLY IN THE GO ZONE.

THE GO ZONE IS AT AUDIENCE EYE LEVEL.

We're all trying to talk, but few people actually hear what we are saying. Stay in the GO ZONE and people will not only hear but also remember what you say.

Every time you open your mouth to say something, *the obligation is on you* to ensure that you are heard. In *The Articulate Executive* I outlined a strategy to make that happen. But now I'd like to take a further step and explore the higher implications of the communications experience.

This experience is intimate.

In fact, the relationship between speaker and audience is like sex—intimate, thrilling, rife with adventure and danger. Most speeches are charged with psychic energy that, once spent, can leave the speaker elated but soon exhausted. Like a sugar rush, or sex, the wave of energy spikes, then fades rapidly when the deed is done.

The relationship between speaker and audience is like sex.

To bridge the large gap between how we present ourselves and how we *could* present ourselves, between what we say and how people *perceive* what we say, between mediocrity and excellence, we need only reposition our minds:

Old thinking: What a chore ... I'll just do what I've seen other people do. . . . This is no fun, I can't wait for it to end. . . . Maybe I can get through this without humiliating myself. . . . I'm boring. . . . This is terrible. . . . I'm doing badly. . . .

New thinking: This is fun, it's creative. . . . I'll try some new things. . . . I'm actually enjoying this. . . . How good can I be? . . . How much value can I give these people? . . . I'm doing well. . . . This is pretty good.

The speaking game is like taking up a new sport. The better you get, the more fun you have. The more fun you have, the closer you come to excellence.

Achieving excellence involves three easy steps. The first step is to make sure you've got the basics in place (you'll recognize Churchill here):

P	*Punch.*	Strong start.
O	*One theme.*	One message only.
W	*Windows.*	Provide concrete examples to enliven your talk and give evidence to back up the main point you're trying to make.
E	*Ear.*	Keep it strictly conversational.
R	*Retention.*	End strongly.

In the case of this book's message:

P   *Punch.* The proposition that most of us never reach our potential—but each of us has it in our power to exceed that potential.

O   *One theme.* Same as *punch.*

W *Windows.* These are illustrations, stories, fables, anecdotes, data, specifics, and other facts to support the proposition.

E *Ear.* A nice, conversational approach that is easy to read.

R *Retention.* An ending that sums up the meaning of the book and leaves people with advice they can use. Certainly I would want to make the point in P and O one last time.

This is a format that, as you can see, I call the POWER formula. Most good speeches and presentations conform to these guidelines, the core elements of CVA and the fundamental building blocks of your presentation or speech. Without them, whatever you say is by definition consigned to mediocrity (slow start, fuzzy theme or no theme at all, few or no concrete examples, gobbledygook language, insipid ending).

That's the first step. Make sure you've got your foundation right.

The POWER formula means greater CVA. Greater CVA means more productivity. More productivity means higher revenues.

The second step is to make certain you know your subject, make sure you take a leadership position, and make sure you practice.

The third step is the most sublime and the most interesting. The third step, once you master it, can transport your audience into a reality you choose.

The third step involves the powers of the mind. This is the connection between the brain and the mouth, not only on an intellectual level but on a higher plane as well. At this level you are really talking from the heart to the heart.

This is a special intimacy, indeed.

Any act of communication, especially from the heart, is a gift. You have no business talking to people if you don't first take care that what you say will add value (CVA) to their professional or personal lives. You are entrusted with the obligation to add value.

First, instead of simply listing, chronicling, or reviewing, figure out the big picture. Understand the larger, economic or historic implications of what you're saying, then cast the whole thrust of your presentation along those lines.

Every time you teach, enlighten, or clarify you bring a gift to your audience.

Let's say you're an investment banker trying to interest a bank in becoming a silent partner in a big M&A deal. Rather than begin with a review of both companies' financials and a recent history, say, of the two entities' business activities, start off with the big picture.

Tell me, for example, that what we have here is a very good fit—for three different reasons. Tell me why that fit comes at a particularly auspicious time not only in the economic cycle of the country but also in the business cycle of this industry. Then tell me exactly what Company A brings to the party and what Company B brings to the party. Then explain how we can combine the strengths of both sides to form a third Company, C, which will be a lot more powerful than the two separate ones.

Then tell me how this merger will enhance profits, grow market share, streamline productivity, make distribution more efficient, and provide a turnkey operation and a host of new products as well as important brand recognition across the board.

It's not until we reach this point that I want to hear about the financials, business philosophy, strategies, components, and recent business activity of the two companies.

Second, position yourself as a leader. Just having a point of view or a call to action will help you look and sound more like a leader.

Third, design your presentation so it is shorter, yet more effective. Most presentations begin at the beginning when they should begin with the ending—starting with the point, the message, the conclusion right up front. It is important to get the big picture on the table first so that everything that follows has a meaningful context. You'll also lessen the chances of being interrupted or running out of time. This reversal—putting the bottom line on the top line—will not only shorten what you say (you'll get the important stuff out of the way early on, thereby reducing the likelihood of redundancies and tangents), but also you'll be tighter, more focused, and crisper in your presentation. Once you've got my attention by forcefully stating the main business point, then all you've got to do is give concrete examples to back up your point.

> **You are more likely to do business if the people listening see you as a leader.**

Your gift here is that you respect your audience's time constraints. You recognize that people you talk to have busy lives and appreciate any effort you may make to be as effective as possible in as short a time as possible. People are thankful if your efforts contribute to their productivity.

Fourth, be more interesting. Politicians understand better than most the dangers of putting people to sleep. "The worst sin in politics," Richard Nixon said, "is being boring."

In the 1996 presidential race, pundits accused Bob Dole of being dull—mainly because Dole seemed unable to express why he wanted to be president. People wanted more from Dole than the broken record of "It's about the future. It's about America. It's about freedom." But Dole still kept specifics to a minimum, adding just a few new bromides such as, "We believe in decency and integrity, and we ought to make them national policy."

The voters shrugged.

Fifth, make your visual aids work for rather than against you. Even acknowledged leaders can lose their power if they allow themselves to be overwhelmed by their own visual aids. Nothing demeans a speaker or leader more than a slide show that's poorly designed and badly executed. To make sure this doesn't happen to you, I'd like to elaborate on some important points we mentioned briefly in Chapters 2 and 3:

1. *Never begin or end your presentation with visual aids.* These include slides, overheads, and computer-generated displays. Stand alone without any props, and begin with a personal story, say, or an anecdote to make a business point. (The exception here would be to start with a montage of slides, or a videotape—never speak while they roll.) At the end, stand alone again without props or visual aids and tell the audience what you want them to take away.

> **The higher in the organization you are, the less you should use visual aids.**

2. *If you use slides, overheads, or computer displays they should occur only in the middle of your presentation, and* *you should use no word slides at all*. (Use the word slide hard copy as notes for yourself, or hand the word slides out later as hard copy—but don't bore your audience by asking them to read while you talk.)

3. *Try to tell and show, rather than show and tell.* Sum up the business point of your *next* slide while the *old* slide is still up—that is, don't show the next slide until you've first introduced it. If you are using only a few slides and showing them separately, introduce each slide before the projector light goes on and before the slide appears on the screen. When you turn the light off, consider throwing out a "takeaway" line—a phrase or two that will help the audience remember the point (". . . and you can expect to see those automobile markets grow, especially in Asia.").

4. *The higher in the organization you go, the less you should use visual aids.* Ideally, the organization's leader would use no visual aids at all—because he or she *is* the show and any distractions would only prove demeaning.

All these tips can help anyone come across as a leader.

As for the pope, no one expects John Paul to resort to slides, overheads, or computer-generated displays. But if he would just throw away his prepared texts, never read another speech, and spend more time in the "Go Zone," I am certain he would experience closer communion with his flock, especially young people.

Whoever you are, your gift is CVA. The result will be greater retention, a more rewarding experience for listener and speaker alike, and the appreciation and downright gratitude of your audience.

> **Beware "perceptions of time." Pauses feel long. But professional speakers use pauses effectively—and a pause that may seem like an eternity to the speaker will feel normal to the audience.**

CHAPTER
TEN

How to Connect
with Yourself

Barbara Bel Geddes once told me that the business of acting is a *shared* experience between the performer and the audience. That's why she liked Broadway better than the movies. Something wonderful happened, she said, when the script was good, the actors clicked, and the audience was just right. When everything came together, a magic unfolded on the stage that gave her a sense of fulfillment and well-being, which she likened to a spiritual experience.

I'm not suggesting that you act out a role when you speak—unless you've had drama training or feel particularly adventurous. Better to just be yourself, have something to say worth listening to, and speak from the heart. But I am saying that speaking *is* a performance, like it or not, and that we are judged on how well we perform—and that the connection between speaker and audience can yield surprising moments of spiritual and emotional benefit to both.

Just be yourself, have something to say and speak from the heart.

Anyone who has ever "been on a roll" in front of an audience—not an imagined roll, but a real one, in which the audience is spellbound—knows what I am talking about. A knowing exchange occurs, a kind of epiphany, and great moments emerge, just as in a play. The speaker reaches down into the Primal Mind I talked about earlier—the emotional and visceral—just as the audience collectively settles into the universal Primal Mind, and the result is as if the jungle drums suddenly kicked in and all the hearts in the place started beating together. Then you are driving to your peak, and just at the right moment, it's all over. Then there's the brief, tense moment of silence and the sudden explosion of applause, and there is no sweeter sound in all the world. (I am reminded of Luciano Pavarotti after singing his heart out for an appreciative audience.) For a while you continue on this astonishing high, and it is only later that you realize you are drained, exhausted, as if someone had pumped out part of your soul.

Think of Patrick Henry in that Virginia church (see Chapter 4). Patrick hit the heights and took his spellbound audience with him. They went up together and came down together in one great unified sigh.

Some will draw the analogy to sex here, and there is some truth to that. Not as wonderful as sex, perhaps, but certainly in the same ballpark. However, the only touching and feeling we're talking about here is purely spiritual.

The speaker, the audience, the occasion, the place, the time, and other factors all offer a wide range of possibilities. But even the "low end"—the "numbers" portion of a senior management analysis presentation, for example—should never again be an excuse to "just give the numbers." In every case, with every presentation, there is a hidden, higher message or opportunity. At the very least, we owe it to our listeners to try to find that larger message.

> **Resist the temptation to just "give the numbers."**

Seek the higher ground, then commit yourself to that message. Try to enlighten, be helpful, teach. Forget about how you are doing. Think only about your message and your audience—Are they getting it? Am I being clear?—and you'll never have to worry about how you are doing. Dive right into the river and go with the current. Once you're in the flow, something curious and unexpected may happen.

Let me explain.

When I was a young TV news producer in New York, I used to try to write books on weekends and days off. Each night I would go to bed with my head bursting with things I wanted to write in the morning. I would wake up at the crack of dawn, eager to get my thoughts on paper—so eager that I would leap out of bed in the gloom and run naked to my writing desk at the other end of the apartment. I would switch on the light and glance at my clock as I sat down to work at 6 A.M. I would pour my ideas onto a legal pad.

Seemingly seconds later I would hear a knock at the door. It would be my wife, who suffered gamely for years through these passionate but not always productive bouts of creativity. She'd ask, "Do you want anything for lunch?" Startled, I'd look at the clock. 12 noon. She'd slide a sandwich under the door—actually, the sandwich would suddenly appear in front of me and just as suddenly disappear as I wolfed it down. Back into the river. On a roll, creative heat flowing out of my hand and onto the page—page after page. Like a fish in the river now, swimming, looping, spinning, playing. Almost like a dream, rushing down, down the river.

"Do you want anything for dinner?" What? It's Pat again. Dinner? I look at the clock. 8 P.M. What? How can it be? Five minutes ago it was noon. What's happening?

A plate appears and I eat while I'm writing, and now it's a couple of minutes later: midnight.

"Are you coming to bed?"

What?

"Are you coming to bed?"

Bed? What time is it?

"Midnight."

Midnight? How can it be midnight?

What's this all about?

What this is about is what the Japanese call satori and the Hindus call dharma. Satori is a kind of altered state of consciousness that kicks in when human beings reach their maximum creative potential. Satori is also a higher plane of reality accessible through prayer, hypnosis, deep meditation, even narcotics. Dharma is when you find your life's work and achieve spiritual bliss by practicing that work to the limits of your ability. Both satori and dharma are characterized by the disappearance of time.

> **Satori kicks in when people reach their maximum creative potential.**

Most of us achieve various levels of satori at heightened moments of intense involvement—usually when we uncork our pent-up powers of creativity, usually beginning at an early age. A small child gleefully attacks her first crayon coloring book. She's mesmerized by the bright colors, the loopy lines, the undiluted ecstasy of watching her hand make something pretty where before there was nothing. Her mother marvels that she stays busy and quiet "for hours"—when in fact the child has no concept of the passage of time. For her, time does not exist.

And that is the indication of the presence of satori. It is literally true that time flies when you're having fun. When you're in satori time passes so fast that everything blurs. Time appears to stand still, even to evaporate altogether.

It is said of Michelangelo that he hardly bothered to

eat or sleep while painting *The Creation* on the ceiling of the Sistine Chapel. Of Einstein, it is said that he would ponder for days over a mathematical equation, sequestering himself from the outside world and distractions. Mozart's creative frenzy in the last months of his brief life sucked him into a runaway altered state of consciousness—a satori—so overwhelming that his exhausted body couldn't take the twenty-two-hour days anymore. He simply wore out, sickened, and died.

Because speaking can be such an intense experience, speakers often find themselves in one degree of satori or another—yet don't even know it. They are aware only that they have no idea where the last twenty minutes went. The difference between a speaker and a leader is often satori. The speaker just speaks. The leader achieves satori.

This satori, this magical contact with the audience is infrequent but available to all of us. The closer you feel to your audience and your message, the closer you come to the altered state. Once in that altered state you may not even remember what you have said. I have heard countless speakers marvel at the loss of memory they suffered, but be equally surprised at the thunderous applause they received when they finished.

Is satori a spiritual experience? I think so. Is it an emotional experience? Definitely. Can it be a religious experience, somehow bringing us closer to God? I have no idea. But I do know that satori and dharma are good, a sign that you are doing something—maybe many things—right. And I do know that everyone who comes away from a satori speaking experience feels good inside, as if they have made a contribution to the world, added some value to people's lives, upped the level of consciousness in their immediate spheres of influence. There's a give and a take on both sides of the satori equation that transcends individuals and, at the risk of sounding spacey, touches the cosmic and pries open the door to something utterly unknowable but altogether desirable.

Every time GE's Jack Welch speaks to his own people, he seems to experience satori.

Every coach in the NFL has probably experienced satori more than once.

Old-time Baptist preachers know a lot about satori.

So when you speak, seek satori. Be utterly selfless— give everything you've got to try to enlighten and inspire your audience. Worry not at all about how you are doing, but care deeply about what you are saying. Forget about yourself. Commit yourself utterly to your message. See yourself as a person on a mission. Be a teacher. Share your wisdom. Advance your point of view. Illuminate the whole room. Do this and there is no measuring how far you can go, or how often you can surprise yourself as you continue to expand and grow.

Hit Satori and you won't have to look for CVA.

CVA will find you.

Silence is the experienced speaker's best friend.

CHAPTER
ELEVEN

How to Profit from the Unexpected

Few things in life get our attention faster than the unexpected. Leaders who understand this psychological truth can jump-start their CVA and capture audiences at a stroke.

When Allen Wheat, president of CS First Boston, spoke to the IBM sales force, he got their attention—and to their delight they got more than they probably expected.

Wheat began with a wake-up call about where Wall Street was headed. He didn't give them a lot of inane amenities, and he didn't spend a lot of time telling them what he was about to tell them. Instead, he got right to the quick: "The success of the entire financial services industry depends . . . to a degree that may surprise you . . . not on people like me—but on people like you," he said right off the bat.

The IBMers were understandably surprised. At first, they must have wondered what Wheat was talking about.

"We've entered into a new era and a new working relationship that didn't exist just a few years ago," he told them.

New era? New working relationship?

Wheat went on to say that Silicon Valley and Wall Street had moved to the same slab of real estate in cyberspace. High tech and financial services were no longer engaged in a client-customer relationship but rather locked in "a new situation that I can only describe as a partnership," he said.

Wheat was saying that the future of sales lay not in sales but in consulting.

This new partnership meant that CS First Boston would in the future want IBM salespeople to spend more time helping plan strategies and long-term solutions and less time trying to sell this program or that computer.

"We need you to help us add value for our clients and customers," he told them. "We need you to make us faster, smarter, more productive and more competitive. . . . We've got to work closely with people in technology, consult with you, seek your expertise, bring you inside, actually make you part of us.

"In other words, we've got to look at you and other technology leaders as partners."

The IBM salespeople, who were expecting just another humdrum speech from another Wall Street suit, listened up.

Wheat was saying something intriguing: *Don't just sell us stuff. Help us be better at what we do.*

This is the value-added part of every transaction that real-estate agents, for example, have known about for years. When people move to a new community, they're looking for more than just a house. They're looking for essential advice. They want to know where they can find a good plumber, doctor, carpenter, painter. They want to know about the schools and churches and clubs. They want a good pharmacist, florist, caterer, all the rest. And they want their real estate person to deliver all this good stuff on the same plate as the home. So the secret to successful real estate often is not sales but consultancy—an unspoken arrangement in which the agent adds value by also serving as an informative resource.

In that sense, Wall Street is not unlike the real-estate business—or any other service business, for that matter. But it takes someone of vision to recognize change in progress, then to articulate that change to inspire action.

> **Help people see things in a new way.**

After Wheat had finished speaking, the IBMers went home thinking about Wall Street—and their own jobs—in an entirely new way.

That's CVA.

Still, many business leaders deliberately shun the mixed blessings of fanfare and attention that life in the public eye affords. They are content to do what they know they do well without all the noise. Usually they don't know they are missing a great opportunity.

But when they discover that moving into the spotlight can have a salutory effect on their business, they also discover that active leadership can be not only productive but also fun. Part of the fun comes from targeting and then exploiting the unexpected to advance your message, your business, your industry, or yourself.

> **Some business leaders don't realize that they are missing opportunities when they remain silent.**

Seeing an improvement in the bottom line is only part of the reward. The rest is realizing that you can make a difference and be an agent of change for the good.

John Mack, president of CS First Boston's rival Morgan Stanley, never cared about the limelight. He rose through the ranks like the sun in the morning, finally winding up at the top of his game. Along the way, he developed a reputation as a friendly but forceful leader who could inspire the troops and get the job done. But John never seemed to care much about turning his gifts of leadership and powers of persuasion to the outside world—preferring instead to keep his eye on the internal affairs of the company.

It wasn't until he appeared on the cover of *Business Week* that he began to step into the sphere of serious public scrutiny. And that's when he began to see the real dollar value of visibility harnessed wisely.

The *Business Week* cover story heralded a bold new direction that Morgan Stanley had chosen to pursue—an adventurous thrust into the as-yet-untested financial frontiers of the Third World. Mack saw opportunity where many others had only seen obstacles. He struck decisively while much of Wall Street dawdled. The first to market generally commands the market. Take the lead and you are likely to keep the lead (witness the *National Enquirer,* still first in a furiously competitive field of tabloid imitators). Mack gambled, and the jury is still out. But he got the world's attention. And if he's right, the world will see him as a visionary.

For many others the question of Third World investment was a quagmire of uncertainty and risk. But for Mack, the situation could not have been more clear. As early as 1992 Morgan Stanley began investing heavily in countries such as Indonesia, Mexico, and China. In India alone, the company spent more than $25 million and installed scores of shock troops in a financial assault on the Indian subcontinent.

"It's grow or die," Mack said simply. "The biggest risk is not to invest." Mack took his message to his own people, honing their interest to a sharp, competitive edge. By the time Morgan Stanley's thrust in new directions got the full attention of the business community, they were already well on their way to a commanding lead in overseas financial markets.

> **Leaders understand the need to take the message to the people—personally.**

By contrast, Michael Spindler (known as the Diesel), the German-born former CEO of Apple, kept his head down, his mouth shut, and seemed to have no ideas and no vision whatsoever as the once-great, even revolutionary company that he took over in 1993 sank toward oblivion. Reportedly distracted by illness in his family and fears that the pressures of the job and brutal sixteen- to eighteen-hour days might trigger a heart attack, Spindler appeared to outsiders to be frozen in inaction. (To be fair, Spindler was confronted by serious short-term and long-term problems he inherited from his predecessor, John Sculley, who went on record saying, "I sometimes wonder if anyone can manage Apple.")

Shareholders were hoping for something unexpected— a burst of brilliant leadership—and still Spindler kept to himself.

What came to pass—or failed to come to pass—was woefully predictable. The silence from the corporate office was disheartening.

Meanwhile, Sun Microsystems was pressing to take a big bite out of Apple, maybe even buy the whole company. Sun eventually lost interest and backed off. But under pressure from bad press, Wall Street, and frustrated shareholders, Apple's exasperated board booted their CEO and installed one of their own in the top spot. "The Diesel" was toast—in large part because if he had ever had any ideas about how to revitalize, re-vamp, or restore Apple to its former greatness, he had never effectively articulated those ideas to his employees, providers, customers, partners (such as IBM), or his own board.

Spindler was gone, and the jury is still out on Apple.

Leadership leads to vision, and articulation leads to action.

Articulation is the spark that ignites action and makes things happen.

For example, articulation in the middle and lower levels of organizations gives self-starters, "high pots" (high-potential people), team leaders, and others career-boosting opportunities.

Take the case of engineer Ellen Storrs, floor manager in a plant that makes toasters, washing machines, microwave ovens, and other household appliances.

With no more R&D money left in the budget and everybody around her discouraged, Ellen did what she had always done in tough situations: She took charge and started to make things happen anyway.

Bypassing her company's unreliable and sluggish information channels, she got direct feedback from customers and even competitors.

Then she took that eye-opening information to motivate her fellow workers and middle managers, saying things such as, "Look, our customers think our work is

111

second best" and "The competition is beating our ass" and "Are we going to just lie down and quit when we're already halfway there and we've got a choice to beat everyone to market?"

That's what she said when she wanted behavioral change. When she wanted speed he just said to hell with it and told people what to do.

Ellen is what behavioral psychologists call a change leader. She's a bit of a rebel and nonconformist who cares a lot about results and not so much about how she gets them. She's like an in-house hired gun who—often with senior management's blessing—cuts loose from traditional methodology to do whatever it takes to get the toughest jobs done.

Yet Ellen may never get to be a top officer in her company. She's an engineer with production line experience, a lot of technical expertise, but no business school. In fact, she's not even a candidate for promotion into the top ranks. She's not particularly good at playing politics and happily admits she's no diplomat. She's even been known to refer to herself as a "worker bee."

But what Ellen brings to the party is priceless. She's a workaholic, but also an effective "people person" who can get the troops motivated to accomplish the near-impossible. Her real genius is her ability to inspire people to accomplish more than they thought they could do—and do it faster and better as well.

So when her boss sees a tough assignment, he invariably gives it to Ellen. More than once the boss was delighted to discover that Ellen was *already* hard at work on the problem even before it came to his attention.

Ellen has probably never heard of CVA, but she certainly understands how it works.

Halfway across the country, Cary Potts sells personal care products for one of the world's largest consumer products companies. Ten years ago they called him a salesman. Next they called him a salesperson. Last year they were calling him an "associate." But today they're telling Cary that from now on he should think of himself as a "category manager."

Category manager?

From now on, Cary Potts wasn't going to be selling shampoo to big wholesale customers such as Kmart and Wal-Mart—at least not like in the old days. Now the idea was to help the big stores better manage his brand and even *the complete category* of personal care to the advantage of both the store and the entire personal care products industry. The theory here is that when the tide rises, all boats (brands) rise with it.

But this means that Cary is today more than a category manager. Cary—like it or not—is now a consultant. Now he's supposed to use his years of knowledge on the job to create a new working relationship with an old and valued customer. He's not just moving product, filling shelves, and taking orders anymore. These days Cary is helping map marketing strategy, redesign shelf space, engineer product flow, upgrade technology, and all the rest. He spends a lot more time with his customers (now his clients) than he used to, and he's been encouraged by his management to think of himself as an important player in the effort to grow his business. The stores welcome the new arrangement. The wholesalers and Cary have come to see themselves as partners.

Cary is investing a lot more time these days face-to-face with his new partners. And to protect that investment he has had to upgrade his CVA. The new demands of the job have forced him to try to be more effective in meetings, skilled in negotiations, and credible in conversation—altogether more like a business leader (or category leader) every day in every way (a far cry from the old days of just being another salesman).

The payoff comes when the working relationships warm to friendships, short-term turns long-term, traditional business roles overlap, and functions begin to regroup and bond—and the distinctions between work and play start to blur. For people like Cary, the new demands of the economy have allowed him to reinvent himself—unleashing a flood of creativity and imagination the old job definition would never have allowed—and re-create his career (at some companies they call this empowerment).

Part of that re-creation has been a growing recognition of the powers of CVA, and the knowledge that all his ambitions and talent could falter without it.

The only sign that Cary Potts may ever have that his CVA is working for him is the only sign he'll ever need:

Business has never been better, and he's never had so much fun.

> **Leaders give added value by offering more than we expect.**

CHAPTER
TWELVE

Lead by Storytelling

If you want to get people to do your bidding, or do the right thing, or act as a team, it is always better to tell them a story than to tell them what to do.

Nothing works like anecdotes, illustrations, examples, analogies, parables, even fables to make people think. Once people start thinking, they can decide for themselves to take action.

If you dictate, people will respond with their minds. If you lead by telling a story, people will respond with their hearts. Choice without heart, or conviction, is business as usual. Choice based on conviction is an invitation to excellence.

> **One good anecdote is worth more than a raft of ideas. One picture really is worth a thousand words.**

You just never know how far or how high people are able to go until you touch them deep inside. And we don't mean just things sentimental. We're talking about using your powers of leadership to engage people by opening doors, shedding light, and sparking *personal* interest to bring people over the line and into your camp.

Once you unlock the personal in each of us the result can be anything from tears to cheers and an unleashing of human potential so powerful it will surprise you. The key is to let the story be your message.

No one knew this truth better than Christ, who, to the best of our knowledge, never wrote down a single word. Instead, he told parables that changed the world. And if Christ did not actually tell the story himself, his actions spoke better than words—and went on to become stories themselves.

By contrast, the Apostle Paul wrote letters to the Ephesians, Corinthians, and Romans talking about love, redemption, forgiveness, and salvation. Yet ironically— even though Paul wrote out his ideas—most people have no idea what Paul said unless they refer to the Bible.

The difference between Christ and Paul is that Christ spoke with stories and Paul wrote in abstractions.

Abstractions go in one ear and out the other. Stories are forever.

That's why many of us don't remember what Paul said about brotherly love. But Christ gave us the eternal parable of the Good Samaritan, which tells us how to treat our neighbors—without *telling* us how to treat our neighbors.

> **Let your story be your message.**

Most schoolchildren know the story of the Samaritan (a member of a onetime Jewish sect generally despised by other Jews) who came across a man who had been beaten and robbed. The Samaritan not only comforted the man but also secured lodgings for him at a local inn. Lesson: Even if someone reviles you, treat that person with kindness and generosity.

Paul talked about order, discipline, and the sanctity of the law. But Christ recognized that simply to follow rules without understanding the wisdom behind the rules is folly. So when the Pharisees turned the temple into a market for sacrificial animals (to comply with an ancient law requiring that animals be offered at certain ceremonies), Jesus drove the merchants out of the temple and back to the market where they belonged. The story has become legend. Lesson: Don't defile what is sacred.

Paul talked about the glory of personal sacrifice. Christ made the concept of personal sacrifice real when he told the allegory of the pearl merchant who finally discovered the perfect pearl—but was able to afford it only by selling all his other pearls. The merchant gave up a fortune to achieve perfection. Lesson: To find perfection in the spirit, you might have to lose almost everything material.

Paul talked about the desirability of celibacy and the single life. But Christ taught that while the single life might be good for the few, the institution of marriage was better for the many. The Marriage at Cana—in which he

119

spared the bride's family social disgrace by turning water into wine so the celebration could continue—is Christ's first recorded miracle. Lesson: The institution of wedlock is a good thing and should be encouraged.

Corporate leaders understand, as Christ did, that a little tale can go a long way. When PepsiCo president Chris Sinclair spoke at a senior management conference, his message was that we are all capable of a lot more than we think. To make the point he told a story about a twelve-year-old boy growing up in India.

"You see, this boy had a little bout with polio . . . and although his life was never threatened, he did face the real possibility of spending his life in a wheelchair," he said.

"Well, as you can imagine, at first the boy was very upset. He couldn't accept the fact that all his friends were out playing and going to school . . . and there he was standing on a beach trying to learn how to walk.

"But after a while . . . gradually . . . he stopped feeling sorry for himself.

"And he concluded that while his legs wouldn't move, the real problem was in his head.

"Well, he made up his mind that within one year he wouldn't be just walking—he'd be running. And you know what? It happened. . . .

"I know—because I was that little boy."

They got the point.

I heard the same kind of message driven home by another speaker, who told a story about Socrates:

A boy asked Socrates to teach him all he knew. Socrates took the student to a river and pushed him underwater. The boy thrashed and thrashed, and when Socrates finally let him up for air, the boy demanded to know what Socrates was trying to do. Socrates told the boy that when he wanted to learn as badly as he wanted to breathe, he would learn.

No doubt the boy got the point. And so did the audience. (Presumably the boy was Plato.)

I listened to a speaker recently who was trying to make the point that if you want to build a company of leaders, you've first got to get people committed to their work and to the company. To do that, you've got to throw out traditional hierarchies and let people pursue what interests them. To clarify, he talked about W. L. Gore & Associates, the company that makes Gore-Tex, a high-tech fabric that lets sweat out without letting wind, rain, and cold in.

"We don't manage people here," the speaker quoted Gore. "They manage themselves." No big titles. No official authority. No real bosses. A machine operator, for example, got bored with his job and wanted to try something else. So he went into product development, soon engineered a new product, and quickly wound up manager for the new product line. That's the kind of associate, Gore said, who not only enjoys contributing to the enterprise but also likes to assume responsibility—the kind of person who seems to rise naturally to leadership.

Another speaker was making the point that most people spend too much time trying desperately to find what they've already got. He talked about the reportedly true story of a South African miner who quit his job and home to go off and find his own diamond mine. He searched for years without success—only to return home and discover that the property he used to own was now itself a thriving diamond mine.

> **To create leaders, you've first got to get people to care.**

The notion of never losing sight of your goal was brought to life by one speaker who talked abut Jack Kennedy's ten-year space program to put a man on the moon. At the outset, the engineers, scientists, and planners had little idea how they were going to get to their destination. They didn't know what the spacecraft would look like and had no concept of the major role computers would eventually play in the project. But they had fierce national pride, a strong sense of teamwork, and unshakable drive. They kept at it, routinely overcoming daunting obstacles—and in the end landed a man on the moon a year ahead of schedule.

Sick and tired of Mickey Mouse rules that stifle your productivity and creativity?

I once heard a story of an engineer who needed a battery for his calculator to finish an urgent project. But when he went to his company's supply people for a battery replacement, they told him that to save money, the company had stopped supplying batteries. If he needed a new battery, he'd have to order one. Delivery would take about a week. The engineer couldn't wait, so he raced to town, bought a battery, and finished the project on time.

Then he submitted an expense voucher for $3.84 to buy a new battery, plus $2.25 for use of his own car. The voucher went out in triplicate, and the company's frustrated comptroller calculated that in the end, the battery cost $30 in processing expenses to the company.

The engineer had simply Mickey Moused the company right back, and the dumb rule was dropped.

Want to push down responsibility and power all the way from the boardroom to the mailroom?

One company discovered that its receptionists were insulting existing clients and potential clients by appearing ignorant and indifferent.

To remedy the problem—which could cost the business millions—the president sent the company jet around to pick up division receptionists and treat them, at corporate headquarters, to a two-day seminar run by a consultant who specializes in training receptionists. They were greeted by the president himself, made to understand the importance of their jobs, lodged in good hotels, and after each day's work taken to fine restaurants.

The personal attention and thoughtful treatment paid off. Today the company claims it has received no further complaints. Now the president says he hears only compliments about his receptionists—and business has never been better.

Want people to act fast?

How Chrysler Corporation reintroduced convertibles

into its model year is a story about fast action. Cruising around Detroit one day, Lee Iacocca spotted someone driving a Mustang convertible. Iacocca decided Chrysler needed a convertible, too. So he called his chief design engineer, who advised Iacocca that it would take five years to get a model to market.

"You don't understand," Iacocca said. "I want a convertible today!" He ordered his people to cut the roof off a sedan and put on a convertible top. He got the car that afternoon and spent the rest of the week driving the new "convertible" around town. People loved the car, and a convertible was on the drawing boards a few days after that.

Want to get people to keep it simple?

Tell about how Thomas Edison used to hire new engineers. The great inventor handed job applicants a lightbulb and asked them how much water it would hold.

Some applicants spent hours trying to determine the bulb's interior space with complex measurements and calculations.

Other applicants simply filled the bulb with water, then poured the water into a measuring cup.

Edison always hired the engineers who kept it simple.

Do managers exist to serve or to be served?

Consider the story of the women who complained to their manager that the toilet seat in the ladies' room was very loose. The manager dutifully submitted the repair request through channels to his maintenance people.

Two weeks later the women were back saying the toilet seat still had not been fixed. So the manager grabbed some tools, knocked on the door of the ladies room to make sure no one was inside, then got down on his knees and repaired the toilet seat himself.

Want to talk about quality?

The Air Force has a policy that people who pack parachutes periodically have to make jumps. The Air Force does not have a quality control problem with chute packing.

Want to talk about trust?

How about the story of the company that runs its cafeteria on the honor system. Armstrong Machine Works has no locks on its sandwich and soft drink vending machines, no cash registers, and no cashiers—just an open coin box. The company reports that they've never had a shortfall, and that on a typical day the coin box will be filled with well over $100.

There are a million stories and a million messages. Each of us is a treasure chest of stories. You need only remember that if you want people to pay attention, recall what you said, and act on your words—and if you want the stature of leadership, make it your business to be an engaging storyteller.

Stories, parables, and fables are all food for the mind—as long as they are used to advance specific messages. If you don't like stories, you can use personal anecdotes, or illustrations out of books, magazines, or TV. The great motivators of history have understood this secret—and now it can be your turn to use it to your advantage.

> **Think less about how you are doing and more about what you are saying.**

CHAPTER

THIRTEEN

Fuzzballs, Hardballs, and Touchstones: Making Contact

Amazing but true: A surprising number of CEOs are "so absorbed in what they want their company to be" that they forget to tell their workers about it.

Mistakenly, they cook up the corporate vision, frame it, hang it on the boardroom wall where nobody looks at it—and then forget about it. A few CEOs even go so far as to argue that they don't need to communicate their visions.

"The average run-of-the-mill Joe could care less if my 'vision' is to dominate the clothing market," says Timothy Finley, CEO of Jos. A. Bank Clothiers, Inc. "They want their paychecks and fair treatment." "In the real world," he says, "people don't think ahead more than six to eight months."

Mr. Finley may have a point—and no doubt gets what he expects. But what if he were to expect—demand— more? What if he made everyone feel they had a personal investment in their work, feel like part of a great enterprise, feel like they were having more fun, like players on a championship team?

What if? What if Vince Lombardi hadn't been the Packers' coach? Would a bunch of so-so players have wound up as NFL champs?

We often see that great leaders' words and actions resonate with their people. That's what makes them great and what helps to make their people great.

They do that by getting personal. The way they get personal is to be relevant. Getting relevant means clarifying the abstract and making the fuzzy concrete. Leaders are good at taking raw information and general concepts and turning them into useful knowledge. Sometimes inspirational knowledge. And sometimes inspirational knowledge that's recast as wisdom.

But whatever they do, great leaders are seldom boring and never mushy.

Put all this together and you've got CVA.

Getting relevant means clarifying the abstract and making the fuzzy concrete.

The late, great Alabama football coach Bear Bryant was controversial but certainly not forgettable. When asked what kind of football player he liked on his teams, Bear was straightforward. He didn't say he wanted good athletes with a lot of heart and determination. Instead, according to *Los Angeles Times* sports columnist Jim Murray, Bear said something like: "If you got any milk-drinking, book-learning, suit-wearing students who can throw a football, you send them to Stanford. If you got any whiskey-drinking, women-chasing, fistfighting athletes who can knock your jock off, you send them to ol' Beah!"

Thank you, Bear. We'll keep that in mind.

Like him or not, Bear Bryant led championship teams, made a mark on an era, and became a legend in his own time.

Gordon Bethune is no household word. But Bethune, who's president and CEO of Continental Airlines, knows how to get things done—and he uses a good lick of CVA every chance he gets.

"The world is full of people with ideas who can't get shit accomplished," says Bethune in his disarmingly direct style.

Bethune is a self-confessed glutton for action who drives a motorcycle and sometimes takes delivery of new Boeing aircraft, flying them to Continental's Houston headquarters himself.

Within two years of taking the helm at Continental in the mid-'90s, he was credited with turning the airline around.

The way Bethune gets things accomplished is one-third inspiration, one-third perspiration, and one-third motivation. To inspire workers, he launched a monthly bonus for placing in the top five in on-time rankings. Then he started shooting for the top three (an extra $65 any month the airline hits the target and $100 if it's number one). An incentive plan for the top twenty executives pays off quarterly—but only if the whole group hits its budget targets.

But Bethune doesn't let memos or e-mail do his talking for him. When there's a job to be done, you'll find the boss right down on the floor with the mechanics and flight attendants and baggage handlers pressing the flesh, sharing his ideas, discussing his strategy, telling people why he's doing what he's doing, and eliciting their support.

He always gets it.

With his managers, he's a straight-talking, straight-shooting guy who never misses an opportunity to encourage a good idea or get everybody rallying around the same flag.

Great leaders are never boring.

The value added that Gordon Bethune brings to the party is the same value added you'd get if you mounted a jet engine on a pickup truck. When the jet kicks in, instead of cruising the freeway, you're riding a rocket sled. Gordon Bethune is the jet engine that started pushing Continental down the right road in a hurry.

Becoming a legend or just getting seriously in touch with people means getting personal and relevant. To do that, you've got to translate the abstract (let's call it the Fuzzball) into the concrete (call it the Hardball). The key to the Hardball is relevant reference (we'll call this one the Touchstone).

The personal and the relevant are two of the brightest facets of CVA.

Here are a few quick examples:

Fuzzball: MIS is being redesigned (passive voice, which only makes it weaker) to enhance productivity, client response time, and office efficiency.

Hardball: We're taking out our two mainframes. Everybody's getting one desktop and one laptop. The new satellite internal web will let us talk to our partners in China in real time twenty-four hours a day. And if you have to get an immediate answer to a problem or share information for wing design changes, all you have to do is click on-line.

It's okay to include the fuzzball in your presentation—as long as you go on to add the hardball (as in the example above).

Examples are *touchstones*.

The *hardball* helps provide *touchstones*—mainframes, desktop, laptop, internal web, China partners, twenty-four hours, wing design changes, on-line—which make it possible for everyone to identify with what the speaker is trying to communicate.

Here's more:

Fuzzball: Implement strategic advantage to grow market share and interface corporate disciplines.

Hardball: We've got a six-month jump on the competition with our new color document processor, the PV-100. So we're moving quickly to slash introductory prices, set up distribution in China and India, launch promotional golf and tennis marketing deals with our IBM partners, advertise heavily during the Winter Olympics, and work closely with people from the factory in Taiwan to coordinate manufacturing and distribution.

Touchstones: six-month jump, PV-100, China, India, golf, tennis, IBM, Olympics, factory, Taiwan.

Fuzzball: We must redefine our market niche and prioritize available research initiatives to impact sales and distribution.

Hardball: We tried, but failed, to get a foothold in the pocket pager market for medical doctors. So we're now going after a wider market: doctors plus home care workers, nurses, and Emergency Medical Service people. The wider market will carry higher distribution and marketing costs, but we expect to triple sales in eighteen months.

Touchstones: Pocket pager, doctors, home care workers, nurses, Emergency Medical Services people, eighteen months.

Fuzzball: We will enhance productivity, sharpen efficiencies to improve quality, increase revenues, and strengthen shareholder value.

Hardball: We're combining engineering, manufacturing, marketing, and customer service under one roof to make sure customers get the Internet products they ask for. We expect this change will speed IMX software and first-stage Wizard processors to market in half the time and slash returns by 80 percent. Engineering and customer marketing teams will work together for the first time to design TST parallel processing extenders. The combination of new efficiencies we think will boost revenues 9.5 percent in the first year alone. We're already getting favorable reviews from Wall Street.

Touchstones: Engineering, manufacturing, customer service, Internet, IMX software, Wizard processors, 80 percent, TST parallel processing, 9.5 percent, Wall Street.

Fuzzball: It is imperative that we interface human capital with process reengineering to implement an environment of continuous improvement.

Hardball: Right now we're like a Mercedes-Benz sitting in the driveway with no tires. Stargate is a great franchise, but we're not going anywhere until our people start working together as a team. We took out a whole level of management to make it easier and quicker for customers to get good service. We've got the best people in the right jobs, but we're still getting low customer satisfaction evaluations from Sears and Wal-Mart—because we haven't learned to work together. On top of that, some of us simply seem unwilling to believe we can learn or improve. We've got to talk to each other and work together if we expect to get the tires back on the car and get that Mercedes rolling again.

Touchstones: Mercedes-Benz, driveway, tires, management level, low satisfaction, Sears, Wal-Mart, tires, Mercedes.

So strike your fuzzballs, replace them with hardballs, and make sure your hardballs are loaded with as many touchstones as possible. You'll be amazed how much easier it is to score with your audience.

That's CVA.

Instead of talking about what's happened, talk about what you *expect* to happen—then use what's already happened to back up your projections.

CHAPTER
FOURTEEN

Savage Focus: Driving Your Message Home

I watched, fascinated, as a black lab pointed his body long and low like a torpedo, his paw raised slightly off the ground, his eyes focused on a tennis ball in a man's hand. A child hung from the dog's neck, trying to play. At the same time, a yapping little terrier nipped boldly at the lab's rear legs.

Incredibly, the dog seemed not to notice. His gaze locked like radar on the tennis ball, even as the ball whipped back and forth in the man's hand. It was as if there were an invisible wire running from the tip of the dog's nose to the ball. When the man finally threw the ball, the lab took off like a shot, leaving child and terrier sprawling.

Could this be a canine version of satori?

In Africa I watched lions stalk prey with the same relentless single-mindedness. Mind and body were one as the lions inched closer and closer through the tall grass (feline satori?), moving in for the kill.

Few of us experience that kind of intense concentration. But this is exactly the kind of focus required to elevate the average performance from forgettable to memorable.

I'm talking about keeping your eye on the ball, then pursuing your objective straight to its conclusion.

This is a characteristic—like right thinking and passion—we often find in highly competent people who are asked to lead, or who rise naturally to leadership.

> **The key to the great presentation is an unusually high level of focus.**

Scott McNealy, the predatory, cheerful, hockey-playing chief of Sun Microsystems, has boiled his business philosophy down to a snappy set of aphorisms that make his competitors flinch.

"Have lunch or be lunch" is one of his favorites.

"Get all the wood behind one arrowhead" and "To ask permission is to seek denial" are others.

The boyish-looking Sun CEO is an in-your-face kind of guy who sometimes lets his homilies do his talking for him.

Steve Forbes boiled his entire Republican presidential candidacy down to two words: flat tax.

Former Xerox CEO David Kearns can sum up his main mission in life in just one word: education.

Throughout history, people writing and talking about commerce, business, and money have found ways to make thoughts timeless—and pack large concepts into small spaces.

Want to talk about the wrenching effects of downsizings and reorganizations on salaried workers? The KiKuyu (an East African tribe) saying, "When elephants fight it is the grass that suffers" pretty much sums it up.

Want to talk about false advertising?

"There are more fools among buyers than among sellers." (French proverb)

How about tax evasion?

"Gold and love affairs are hard to hide." (Spanish proverb)

Filthy lucre?

"A mere madness, to live like a wretch and die rich." (Robert Burton, England, seventeenth century)

Lawyers?

"The first thing we do, let's kill all the lawyers." (Shakespeare)

Bending the rules?

"What's integrity to an opportunity?" (William Congreve, England, seventeenth century)

Savings?

"There are three faithful friends—an old wife, an old dog, and ready money." (To be politically correct, sadly you might have to rewrite Ben Franklin to make it "old spouse.")

The nature of success?

"I know that unremitting attention to business is the

price of success—but I don't know what success is."
(Charles Dudley Warner, nineteenth century)

Salesmanship?

"It is not from the benevolence of the butcher, the
brewer, or the baker that we expect our dinner, but from
the regard of their own self-interest. We address ourselves
not to their humanity, but to their self-love, and never
talk to them of our own necessities, but of their advantage." (Adam Smith)

Business ethics?

"Here's the rule for bargains: Do other men, for they
would do you. . . . That's the true business precept."
(Charles Dickens)

Skewed values?

"He who is no longer capable of enjoying human hap-
piness devotes himself utterly to money." (Schopenhauer)

Early retirement?

"It is not be any means certain that a man's business
is the most important thing he has to do." (Robert Louis
Stevenson)

The nature of money?

"Money ranks with love as man's greatest source of
joy . . . and with death as his greatest source of anxiety . . .
[it's] equally important to those who have it and those who
do not." (John Kenneth Galbraith)

Struggle against overwhelming odds?

"Working for Warner Brothers is like fucking a por-
cupine: It's a hundred pricks against one." (Wilson Mizner) (Resist the temptation to actually use this one.)

This bit of irreverence aside, the memorable line—the focused thought—can go a long way to driving home your point.

By contrast, a lack of focus or the downright obtuse can be mystifying. No one can better conjure the artfully obtuse than a seasoned bureaucrat. When two masters of obfuscation are together in the same room talking about Fed monetary policy, the results can approach new heights of incoherence—as witness this remarkable exchange between Richard Svon, president of the Boston Fed Bank, and Robert Black, president of the Fed Bank of Richmond.

Mr. Svon: Are you suggesting "slightly" and "might" on the second part, or "somewhat/would" and "slightly/might" in terms of symmetry?

Mr. Black: I was suggesting "slightly/might" on both of them.

Mr. Svon: "Slightly/might" on both?

Mr. Black: Yes. That predisposes us not to move unless we have some evidence that we don't now have. It's a stronger vote to remain where we are than "somewhat" and "would," I think. We may be getting into minutiae here, but . . . if I were voting, I would (accept) "somewhat" and "would." I even toyed with the idea of "somewhat" and "might" and other permutations and combinations of that.

Mr. Svon: "Slightly/would," I suppose.

It can be no wonder that Fed policy, like the finer points of the law, requires a priesthood of cognoscenti to decipher the code. (But whatever policy emerged as a result of this particular exchange could determine how much you're paying for the mortgage on your new house!)

Yet neither you nor I—and even some of the policy mavens themselves—have a clue what all the gobbledygook really means.

On the other hand, when leaders speak, they come at us with a sense of purpose and focus that distinguishes them from other people.

That's why focus (picture Norman Schwarzkopf giving his famous press briefing during Desert Storm) is a hallmark of leadership. But first we've got to have something to focus *on.*

Use the active voice to clarify, the passive to obfuscate.

First, you've got to know what you're talking about. If you're a financial person, you want to leave the finer points of mass marketing to someone else. If you're an engineer, you'll resist the temptation to wax eloquent on investment policy—unless you also happen to be an investment expert. An artist asked to speak on her own work should not venture into the political policy of the United Nations—unless her work is directly influenced by the United Nations and she knows enough about the United Nations to be helpfully informative.

Talking about what you know opens the door a crack. Taking a position on a subject you understand and care about pushes the door open a little farther. Explaining one point and nothing else opens it more. Speaking in pictures—giving vivid examples to help make your point—swings it even wider. Then speaking as if you were having a conversation, with the intimate and personal touch all audiences crave, then wrapping it up with a bang, throw the door wide open.

Remember: Never lose focus on what you're talking about, why, and to whom. Know exactly why you're doing this. More business? Career enhancement? Personal exposure? The sheer joy of teaching? Ego? Money? What's the purpose? What do you want to get out of this? What do you want your audience to get out of this?

> **Most audiences can walk away with only one number.**

In one speech, Microsoft's Bill Gates wanted his audience to leave understanding that making mistakes—even failing—can be a good thing.

"It's fine to celebrate success—but it is more important to heed the lessons of failure," Gates noted. "The message I want a manager to communicate is, I don't blame anybody in particular for this problem. What I care about is how well we rally around to come up with a new approach to resolve it. . . . When employees know that mistakes won't lead to retribution, it creates an atmosphere in which people are willing to come up with ideas and suggest changes. . . . This is important to a company's long-term success. . . ."

Gates talked about his willingness to take risks, but he candidly acknowledged that nobody's perfect.

"I've made some expensive mistakes myself," he admitted. "My blunder was to insist that one of our earlier programs run on the Apple II, a popular but underpowered computer. To make it work, we left out some potential features that required more power. . . . Lotus, a new company at the time, didn't make the same mistake. Lotus 1–2–3 was designed expressly for the then new and more powerful IBM PC. My mistake knocked our spreadsheet Multiplan out of the sweepstakes. . . ."

But this mistake taught Microsoft never to compromise the top end to accommodate the bottom end.

Always on target, not concerned about blame, focusing only on the bigger picture and long-term goals, Gates showed leadership by accepting responsibility and using his own mistake as an example of how to gain from failure.

That was his objective—to give a brief lesson on how to gain from failure.

Once you know your objective, your reality narrows to a single message. You concentrate on that reality, and the message becomes the vehicle that will carry you to your objective. Focus savagely.

That's CVA.

Do your audience a favor and stick to your allotted time.

CHAPTER
FIFTEEN

The Cascade:
Saturating Your Audience

Savage focus is a benchmark of CVA because any audience will benefit from a single-minded, disciplined approach. But to learn how to stay focused, think about the relationship between champagne and gravity.

I remember watching some happy fool in a party hat stack a bunch of champagne glasses into a pyramid, then pour bubbly into the top glass until it overflowed—and kept on flowing like a waterfall, filling all the other glasses. The parlor gag lasted about twenty seconds—until the partymeister tipped into the glasses and the whole thing came crashing down.

While it lasted, the champagne trick was impressive. It put me in mind of a psychological game that good writers and speakers use.

I call it the Cascade.

To give you an example, a client of mine recently

asked me to help him put together a position paper he could use in a series of speeches he planned to make.

So I wrote something like this:

The success of our business in the next century will depend on our ability to go global. . . . Politics, people, cultures, even whole economies are passing back and forth across borders and boundaries with irresistible regularity. . . . Billions of dollars move around the world in an electronic instant. . . . Multinational corporations are beginning to eclipse whole countries in the breadth and depth of their power and influence. . . . Markets are shifting. . . . Buying habits are changing. . . . The labor force doesn't speak English. . . . Tsunamis of change are sweeping the world. . . . That's why corporations that do not become international will eventually no longer be able to compete. . . . Many companies in a crowded field—conceivably even our own—will simply cease to exist.

If these companies no longer exist, then the industry will begin to consolidate rapidly.

With consolidation will come a new wave of shakeouts and mergers.

These shakeouts and mergers will leave perhaps two or three goliaths standing on the bloodied field of battle. . . .

That final battle will be the last stage of an agonizing process that could last well into the twenty-first century—unless we take five specific measures *now* to ensure that the period of suffering is a lot shorter and that we are one of the players still standing when it's all over. . . .

(Then I spelled out the five steps specific to his company.)

If you look back over this little intro, the Cascade doesn't start until the sentence "If these companies no longer exist . . ."

The principle of the Cascade is simple: Begin each new sentence with a spin off the previous sentence. The first line of the new sentence borrows from the last line of the sentence before. One cue word or cue phrase leads to another, in a logical build, something like this:

If we do nothing, we will open the door of opportunity to our competitors. . . .

If we open the door of opportunity, we may never recover. . . .

And if we never recover, we will simply die.

You can see that the preposition "if" comes in handy. Here's another:

We are positioned now to strike. . . .

If we strike now, we beat the competition to the punch. . . .

If we beat the competition to the punch, we gain vast new markets. . . .

If we gain vast new markets, we will dominate the industry. . . .

If we dominate the industry, a lot of our competition will simply go away. . . .

And if much of our competition goes away, we will be positioned at the top in the twenty-first Century.

Of course, if you spoke or wrote like that all the time, you'd sound like you had a mental problem. But if you save your Cascades for the places where you want to press a point, the technique will serve you well. To support your argument in a meeting, for example, the Cascade is very effective.

But there's more: The Cascade can and should also exist within the larger framework of your presentation, speech, or written material. And it should also exist within your head.

> **If you think you have more than one message, make sure the secondary points you want to make serve to amplify your main theme.**

This technique can be illustrated by a pyramid-shaped rocket that might look like this:

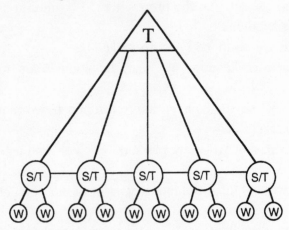

T   = Theme
S/T = Subtheme
W   = Windows (examples to prove your point)

This is what your presentation ought to look like. Just a simple design. A rocket. But notice that this design is streamlined. We've got just one theme, a message. At the same time, we've got five subthemes. You can see that all those five subthemes are tied directly to the main theme. Then we've got a bunch of windows (W) or concrete examples (data, word pictures, illustrations) that will let us see exactly what you base your conclusions on—thereby giving you and your presentation a lot more credibility.

Here's where Cascade 2 comes in. Let's say your theme is "The future of the service industry will depend on how well firms harness and develop their most precious product: intellectual capital. In the future, brains, education, and experience will determine the fate of private enterprise as we know it. . . ."

Okay. That's a pretty clear position. You'll want to back up that position by articulating trends, changes, and developments in progress today that will affect tomorrow. You might discuss these changes in the context of your subthemes. Suppose your subthemes are:

- emerging Third World markets;

- the U.S. shift from a manufacturing to a service-based economy;

- the restructuring and consolidations of whole industries;

- diversity and the need for new skills in the workplace;

- the growing role of industry in the traditional functions of government.

Fine. Now you've got your theme and subthemes. But let's not forget your all-important windows. You can't have too many windows in any presentation. Every chance you get, use a specific example to back up not only your theme but every subtheme, as well. Give examples of Third World markets, the shifts to service, restructuring and consolidations, diversity, and the changing roles of industry and government. Now you've really got my attention. I can see that you know what you're talking about and that you're smart enough to *prove to me* that you're knowledgeable.

But here's the hitch: To get it all exactly right, you must also use the Cascade. This means that you start your presentation with your theme. Get it out on the table. Let your audience know you mean business, that you're not going to waste their time. Your rocket is already launched.

And that's the first cataract (rapids) of the Cascade.

The next cataract is windows or subthemes or both. Even though the rocket has *windows* flowing out of subthemes, you can throw in *windows* anywhere.

So a window might be your next cataract. Or you might use a subtheme. Just make sure that everything refers back to your theme. In other words, *windows* modify *subthemes*, which modify the *theme*. If your theme is intellectual capital and one of your subthemes is strategic planning, you've got to make sure you talk about strategic planning in terms of intellectual capital. In this sense, strategic planning is just another way to talk about intellectual capital. Strategic planning becomes an *aspect* of intellectual capital. Strategic planning by itself, as a separate subject, does not belong in this presentation.

All along, keep reminding me that everything you say, every point you make, is another way of reinforcing your message that the future of the service industry depends on investment in human capital.

> **If you pour your theme all over your presentation, your presentation will saturate your audience.**

Now I can *see* what you're talking about. More importantly, I can *understand* all the connections. All these connections link one concept. This is what the Cascade is all about. It's as if you poured your theme all over your presentation and your presentation saturated the audience.

One theme. Many ways to express that theme. That's how the Cascade works. The Cascade is your way of ensuring that your audience:

1 hears what you say the first time;

2 could pass a quiz on what you said;

3 is likely to take some action.

That's CVA.

To galvanize your audience, try a mixed bag of personal stories, anecdotes, projections, and rhetorical questions.

The Gentle American Samurai: A Leader's Story

The power of CVA is all around us. It's a force for good that changes lives and saves a lot of businesses and jobs. When Tom O'Gorman, president of Glenoit Mills, took over a rival mill in Tennessee, the workforce expected a bloodbath that could leave much of the small town unemployed and without hope.

What they got instead was a good deal and a future that looked brighter than before.

History favored the bloodbath.

The good people of Jacksboro had plenty of reason to fear the worst. Relentless consolidation of the textile industry, rising costs, slackening demand, and cheap imports had conspired to wipe out enough small mill towns in the South to change the face of Dixie forever. Still, the people of Jacksboro had labored through it all, keeping their heads down and their hopes up—praying for an angel but fully expecting a devil.

And when Tom O'Gorman showed up one hot summer afternoon, he more than met their expectations. Some of the people were certain that Satan himself had come to town to steal their jobs and an entire way of life. Maybe even their souls.

After all, look what they thought they were getting: a hard-charging, no-nonsense top industry executive from New York City who—if he was like all those other tough execs from up North—would wipe out the mill workforce with the stroke of a pen, then crack open the champagne and dance on the grave of what had once been a nice little community.

This could have turned out to be the worst kind of carpetbagging. Here was a guy no one knew, or had even met, but whom everyone feared—a destructive force that, like a neutron bomb, could make the people disappear but leave the buildings intact.

They expected the new boss to send goons and suits and lawyers to fire everyone, shut the place down, and lock the gates. Maybe even bulldoze the factory and put up a mall or a theme park. Maybe leave the factory open but run the whole thing with newfangled equipment and fancy computers.

Instead, Tom showed up in shirtsleeves and told everyone that not only would they get to keep their jobs, but they'd also be getting raises.

They expected Tom to turn off the electricity, stop the machines, and throw everybody off the property.

Instead, Tom invited everyone and their families to the first company picnic ever.

They expected to lose all benefits and have to face hard times without a safety net.

Instead, Tom wrote them a benefits package that seemed too good to be true. But it was true.

They expected Tom to act like a carpetbagger—dictate terms and engage in a one-way conversation empty of compassion, understanding, or caring.

Instead, they got a smiling, soft-spoken gentleman with intelligent eyes and a warm handshake. And they were amazed to discover that Tom himself had grown up in a small town not fifteen miles away from that very mill. They were surprised when Tom told them he was one of them, shared the same values, shared the same dreams. He had walked the same red soil, spoke the same language, even knew some of the families. He understood the special charms of homemade pecan pie in an evening, iced tea with mint in the afternoon, smoked ham and greens, good talk on the back porch, crickets singing, and fireflies chasing the stars. From the moment Tom opened his mouth the fears began to melt like butter under a hot sun.

For his trouble—if you want to call it trouble—Tom got more than he had bargained for. He got sharply improved productivity and an eventual steady upward climb in revenues—despite a soft market. Quality control leaped from thirteen returns per hundred to virtually zero, and absenteeism disappeared.

> **Managers always try to do things right. Leaders always try to do the right things.**

It was almost as if an angel had descended upon Jacksboro.

The secret to Tom's success, as he would later relate it, was nothing more complicated than one word: decency. Tom had demonstrated, with his words and his deeds, that CVA in combination with decency and good business ethics can be an especially effective management tool.

Tom's idea was simple: Take a good thing and make it even better. Grow the business with the best business asset he had—the human capital represented by the people who *were* the business.

There were never two opposing sides. It was never "them" and "us." It was always just one team.

It was never dictation. It was always facilitation and conciliation.

It was never about slash and burn. It was always about support and growth.

This is not to say that Tom is not tough. He is. Among other things, he's a level-eyed graduate of Annapolis and one-time Navy captain who has seen power wind up in the hands of people who don't know how to use it. Power wielded by mediocre minds with indifferent talent—insecure operators who eventually brought themselves down by trying to pump themselves up.

Tom understood the proposition that managers always try to do things right, while leaders always try to do the right thing.

Tom always tried to do the right thing—in public as well as in private, in business as well as in his personal life. Consistently doing the right thing translates to one word: integrity.

His integrity led to feelings of high regard, an unheard-of sense of bonding between management and the workforce, and a heightened sense of purpose. Tom understood that it would profit him little to believe in the enterprise if the people down on the floor didn't share that belief or didn't care.

So Tom walked into the cold zone between new management and the workforce and warmed it up with words from the heart that spoke of cooperation and accommodation. He spoke simply and directly, utterly devoid of any trace of insincerity.

Tom said "we."

He said "can."

He said "do it together."

And he tried never to say "never."

But nonthreatening words do not a sissy make. When the numbers faltered several months after the takeover, Tom went face to face with the plant's top managers to make it clear that anything less than goal performance was unacceptable. Then he asked for ideas and input. The question not only came as a surprise to his listeners but also opened minds.

"Tell me what you think," he said. "I'd value your ideas. . . . What has to be done? And what can you and your people do to help make it happen?"

When they reached a consensus, Tom went to the troops and spelled out the updated mission. To listen to him talk, you'd think he had always been part of the plant family. He'd already established himself as a fair-minded, likable straight shooter, so the people listened. In the end, with Tom, the top managers, and the salaried workers all pulling on the same oar, the numbers got right. The mood became so infectious that even the few stubborn holdouts eventually came on board. Quality, productivity, sales, and revenues inched back up.

The ongoing standard of continuing improvement he kept talking about was proving to be challenging, but also a lot of fun.

What made Tom special was not just his business skills but his skills in combination with CVA. Tom's unfailing integrity, manifested in his words, produced new levels of expectation and performance.

Tom's associates in the mill are no more strangers to common decency than the rest of us. They understand that because he did the right thing, they, too, must do the right thing. With ethical behavior, common goals, and the breakdown of barriers between management and the workforce, new lines of communication have opened that made the difference between life and death for one American business inside a whole American industry that is itself under siege. Breaking down traditional barriers to common consensus will be part of the solution for all businesses in the twenty-first century.

That may be the most effective CVA of all.

> **Leaders stand out when they combine ethics, business skills, and CVA.**

CHAPTER
SEVENTEEN

Warriors and Kings: The Roles Leaders Play

Mussolini was a buffoon and a warrior. Hitler was a trickster and a warrior. Dwight Eisenhower, on the other hand, was a warrior and a sage. So was Winston Churchill. Prince Charles is a courtier—even though he may someday be the king of England. Pat Riley, the coach of the NBA's Miami Heat, is more of a statesman and sage than a coach. Convicted evangelist Jim Bakker is a merchant and a trickster. The great Indian chief Tacoma was a priest, sage, and king. Former MIT Business School dean Lester Thurow is a seer. Hollywood producer Steven Spielberg is a priest. Microsoft's Bill Gates is a priest, coach, and seer. Former British prime minister Margaret Thatcher is a warrior and king. GE's Jack Welch is a coach and a statesman. St. Francis was a server.

Everyone you know has characteristics they share with the powerful, the rich, and the famous, characteristics manifested in how they present themselves—what they think and the way they express those thoughts.

Shakespeare's famous line that all the world's a stage will hold true as long as there are people on the planet. Certainly when we step out of the house every morning the curtain, in effect, goes up. Each of us is costumed and uniformed, and each has a role to play. We are required to act a part at certain times every day of our lives, and we all have audiences and critics who rate our performances. If it is your destiny to speak to audiences of any kind, you will play one role or another. If you play no role whatsoever—if you are simply in effect "reading the news" and reporting the facts—you will merely bore.

But if you seek to bring more than just a laundry list to the party, you will find yourself stepping into an identifiable role.

We're all warriors, kings, priests, merchants, tricksters, courtiers, sages, buffoons, coaches, seers, statesmen, conciliators, negotiators, seducers, heroes, victims, worker bees, and more. And we reveal who—and what—we are by how we speak.

But you need not be a man or a woman of the cloth to be a priest, nor wear a crown to be a king.

Innate nobility, dignity, and wisdom determine kings. Shoemakers and cabdrivers can be kings. Kings can also be tricksters. The warrior thinks like a soldier and speaks like a general. The priest opens a door to the mystical and the magical. The merchant is always selling something— even when he's not. The trickster traffics in deceit and lies but is often the most attractive and charming person in the transaction (in time the trickster may not even know that he is a trickster). The courtier serves the king—and may be better educated, more sophisticated, and more articulate than the king himself. The sage is the wizard, the philosopher. The buffoon is the absurd clown who draws laughs of contempt (absurdity sinks to tragedy when a buffoon such as Idi Amin rises to power). The coach is the life guide who encourages us all to stretch ever higher and reach ever deeper. The seer figures out where we are going, then tells us what to expect and how to prepare for it. The statesman, unlike the courtier, who serves the king, is the erudite diplomat who guards his sphere of influence—the leader who shapes policy. The server puts the interests of the common good ahead of his own and tries, not always successfully but always valiantly, to serve us all.

Are you a server? A king? A merchant? A trickster? A statesman? You may never know. But every time you open your mouth, chances are that you will slip into one or more of these categories. And you can be sure that people will subconsciously assign you to one or more of these categories.

> **If it is your destiny to speak to audiences, you will necessarily play one role or another.**

In ancient myths the trickster is always the hero who beats the system and wheedles his way out of trouble and into ascendancy by virtue of his wits, and little else. Brer Rabbit is a descendant of the trickster tradition in myth.

And Bugs Bunny is a descendant of Brer Rabbit. The fox and the coyote also play the trickster in folklore. But a trickster loses his luster when he's more interested in getting into your wallet than staying out of trouble. Public figures who go on television to target the naive and vulnerable, as was the case with Jim and Tammy Bakker, earn and deserve the trickster label.

Buffoons are often larger than life. Sadly, by the time we realize that they are buffoons—and not the brilliant visionaries we thought them to be—they are probably well on the way to self-destruction. In his speeches, Benito Mussolini swaggered like a megalomaniac opera star playing an emperor onstage, but wound up hanging upside down in a market square, where disillusioned Italians spat on his mutilated body. In the late '80s, a well-known Canadian wheeler-dealer nearly brought the retailing industry to ruin when he brashly pasted together a megadeal to buy half a dozen or so premier department stores, including Bloomingdale's, but then couldn't come up with the money. For a short time he could be seen blustering obnoxiously on TV, snapping at reporters, and painting himself as a hero. But then he was forced back into the shadows, where he ended up in bankruptcy—leaving the debris of half-dead companies behind him.

This man's objective was power and money. But his reckless pursuit of both tore a big hole in the fabric of acceptable behavior, and the gods—probably laughing—pushed him off the stage. Exit buffoon.

Was he *all* bad? I don't know, and I don't care. But if

his private life was anything like his public posturing, this is not the kind of guy you would want to have over for dinner.

Chances are, you—like the buffoon—are really many people and many voices. But only one voice can speak at a time. Depending on the business need and the circumstances, we are all likely to fall into one or more of the following categories:

THE SAGE

The sage transcends political considerations and selfish need to provide the kind of prescient wisdom most of us seek—and proves yet again that while intelligence and wisdom go well together, one need not be street smart, or even brilliant, to be wise. The sage strikes the chord of truth and gives the gift of *in*sight to what may be *out* of sight. Historically, leaders have sought the counsel of sages, then often claimed their wisdom for themselves. But unlike leaders and kings, sages do not covet power, nor do they typically abuse it (an exception may be Henry Kissinger, who served as a sage to Richard Nixon but yearned for a crown himself and wound up largely serving himself). The sage builds a career on always doing the right thing (the only thing) and will not budge on principle. For the sage, right thinking must accompany insightful thinking, and the vices of lying and deceit are anathema. Therefore, sages are sometimes at odds with official or corporate policy, because while they may appreciate the need for compromise, they may also loathe expediency.

This means that in business or in life a sage must use all his powers of persuasion to prevail. A sage must be adept at CVA simply to make sure the wrong thing does not come to pass or the right thing is left undone. For example, it will fall to the sage to persuade his peers that the long view may be much wiser than the short view, or that a product not be launched prematurely simply to meet a public relations deadline (remember the 1986 *Discovery* shuttle disaster?), or that cutting seasoned scientists from the research lab to slash costs in the current reorganization is probably not a smart move.

THE PRIEST

The priest, like the sage, is in the business of dispensing wisdom. But the priest's wisdom is dictated not only by morality but also by mysteries beyond our understanding. We entrust our most private selves to our priests, whoever they may be—and a priest or a minion is as eager to welcome us into his spiritual embrace as a politician is to win our vote. But priests, like common men, are flawed—often tragically. Self-deception and outright fraud are not uncommon in this category. When false religious prophets such as Jim and Tammy fall, they fall far and hard, casting a pall of suspicion and doubt on all prophets. So for this reason, and because we live in a world of hard facts, software, and brutal competition, priests must win their stripes just like the rest of us. That's why Steven Spielberg and Bill Gates are both priests. They have ascended to the top of the mountain, where they have seen things the rest of us have not even begun to fathom. Spielberg brought us a special magic that invaded our hearts (*E.T.—The Extraterrestrial,* for example), and Gates helped unlock a universe of knowledge and virtual reality. These people are lesser gods, and that is why we have made priests of them. They see themselves on a kind of evolutionary mission, and we listen because when high priests speak, we have always listened.

Priests seem to have a natural gift for communicating effectively. Their CVA is the practice of enlightenment. The sign of a good priest is that his language will be remarkably simple, his logic compelling, his sentences short and resonant. The priest will not say, "To impact the bottom line of our production targets, we must interface with operations." The priest will say, "If we share our information with the right people we can expect good things to happen." A priest may be a brilliant engineer, but you will know he is a priest because he will see applications the rest of us may not be able to see, and he'll articulate those visions in a way that even the least technical among us can understand.

THE KING

The king is a father figure who unites, heals, and leads. He determines not only policy, but sometimes also morality. The king, like the priest, reaches into the ether and wraps any civic, secular, or business message in terms of loyalty, integrity, and honor. Anyone can talk about these virtues—and many do—but the king contrasts with the trickster, who would be king by practicing what he preaches. The trickster (false king, false prophet) is incapable of honesty and is found out in the end. But the king is truly noble. The king will always attempt to seek the highest good for as many people as possible. But even he cannot serve everyone equally well. When diverse interests clash to restrict his influence, the king will at the very least try to serve well those constituencies to which he is beholden: customers, shareholders, and employees, for example. Arthur Martinez of Sears is such a king. The king's downfall in life as well as in fiction is because human nature often prevails to drag the king off his throne. Kings of weak character, though of noble intent, invariably succumb to the same temptations the rest of us succumb to—only on a much larger scale and with larger consequences.

A king makes for a good leader and a good boss—not because he is by nature lordly, but because he has the interests of his people at heart.

You will know a king when you meet someone who is as gracious as he is powerful. You will know a king when that same person shows frustration when being told something can't be done. A king will gently but firmly dismiss excuses when something is not accomplished.

A weak king will blindly accept a thirty-two-year-old consultant's recommendation of an across-the-board 8 percent personnel cutback in every department to cut costs. A wise king will demand patience and seek the counsel of his most trusted advisers to find a better solution. A strong king will do almost anything to avoid firing his most loyal workers—including absorbing short-term loss, reassigning responsibilities, and finding alternative work. A great king will confound all the experts, fire all the consultants, figure the whole thing out for himself, and go on to conquer a whole industry in spite of over- whelming odds.

The king's CVA is his ability to motivate and lead with words the rest of us find "great" or "inspiring." The king will bring us to our fullest potential and open doors to higher levels of competency in a way that is disarmingly painless. He will make work more stimulating, our work lives richer and more interesting. With help from kings we will achieve our sales targets, meet our numbers, balance our budgets, reconcile our team members, increase our cash flow, earn more money—and have more fun doing these things.

THE TRICKSTER

The trickster is ubiquitous. Like a dormant virus, he inhabits us all, but assumes evil proportions when he blooms into full, venomous flower. The trickster beckons us to inhale the poisonous rose and partake of his black charm, usually in an effort to part us from our money or our principles.

He beguiles us with words like seductive music, then takes his pleasure before we know we've been had (consider Shakespeare's Richard III). Given a choice, the trickster will lie—even when lying is unnecessary—and seems incapable of telling the truth or accepting responsibility. On the other hand, he will rise to grace and play that lofty role with artful dignity if good behavior will serve selfish ends. If unsuccessful, he will resort to his true nature and withdraw—only to regroup and strike again under a different flag and behind a different face. The trickster is the diciest category to navigate, because whenever we sell or woo or cajole or persuade or coax or tease or beg we run the risk, depending on the circumstances, of becoming tricksters ourselves. Paradoxically, the trickster is easy to love and easy to forgive. He is not necessarily the black-caped villain making off with the helpless virgin. More often than not, he may actually be our lawyer, our accountant, our boss, or perhaps—as the U.S. government knows only too well—our ally.

The trickster, unhappily, is a master of CVA, and in the work environment—if allowed to rise unrecognized through the ranks—will bring down more than just himself. President Clinton's partners, Little Rock lawyer Jim McDougal and Arkansas governor Jim Guy Tucker, both convicted of fraud, brought the flame of disgrace and dishonor to the White House in an election year. Both men charmed their way to the tops of their professions with a smooth-talking talent for taking the good-ole-boy confidence game to new heights.

THE WARRIOR

Buffoons such as Mussolini and Amin aside, warriors also can be cordial, gracious, and gentle. The greatest warriors take up the sword for the common good, believe deeply in what they are fighting for, remain calm in the thick of battle, work hard for peace, despise war, claim no personal credit for victory, and understand the flaws and shortcomings of their own human nature. The flinty chip off the old DNA block that makes people like General Dwight Eisenhower (later President Eisenhower) and General Norman Schwarzkopf come alive in times of crisis to assume their mission in life often lies dormant until triggered by events. Amiable Ike loved fishing and golf and might easily have passed for a retired midwestern insurance executive—even after leading the Allies to victory against the Axis in World War II. Norm Schwarzkopf is everybody's favorite uncle and the coach of the local football team. But stir his righteous wrath, as Saddam Hussein did, and you'd better run for your life.

But not all warriors are heroes. The warrior's naturally combative nature can also bring him down. G. Kirk Raab, for example, rose to lead Genentech, but his abrasive personality and repeated charges of conflict of interest finally forced his resignation. The good business warrior balances harsh military single-mindedness with quiet reason, and tempers impatience with determination. He is coldly focused, yet warm; a good commander but an even better listener; opinionated yet thoughtful; powerful yet never a bully.

The CVA of the warrior, like that of the king, is an innate genius for making the complex easy to understand and the unmanageable manageable. A great warrior is not intimidated by adversity—may thrive on it—and has a gift for leading the less courageous against formidable obstacles made to seem less daunting by the inspiring words of the warrior leader.

THE COACH

The coach is driven by a need to improve the world around him. He is gratified when the fruits of intuition produce significant change for the good. By virtue of the fact that he is a coach, he assumes a mantle of experience and wisdom not granted to everyone. At the same time, like the king or warrior, the coach must also assume responsibility when things go wrong. The most successful coaches enhance performance with the natural gift of encouragement so team members can find themselves. Good coaches believe in the rightness of the mission or method and therefore are sometimes accused of allowing ego to stand in the way of results. But when ego is tempered with common sense, understanding, and a willingness to get *out* of the players' way, good coaches can generate not only a higher level of performance, but also add real economic value to any organization.

In the end, the coach helps players unlock their potential to meet ever higher expectations (like GE's Jack Welch). But the more undisciplined the discipline, the easier it is for bad coaches to wind up in positions of leadership—in areas such as personal development, for example, where we are surprisingly likely to entrust ourselves to just about anyone who calls himself a coach. The measure of a coach is simple. Poor coaches produce poor results. The good coach in business first explains (the problem), then instructs (the solution), then inspires (the desire). In the workplace, there is no finer kind of CVA.

THE SERVER

The server lives to helps others. Sometimes the business server—such as Richard Branson, chairman of Virgin Atlantic Airways—is amazed to find that good conduct pays off big-time. Few people in the business have as much fun as Branson, and few give away so much money (or have so much to give). When he's not ladling money out the door (the business server's signature M.O.), Branson is forever dreaming up tantalizing ways to serve his customers (free airport limo and massage service, for example).

Other well-known servers are show biz honcho David Geffen, who gives his time and cash to any number of different causes; and Jimmy Carter, who retired from a well-intended if naive presidency to devote his life to helping build (with his own hands) housing for the poor and disadvantaged. Other servers labor happily in obscurity—like the geniuses who have toiled unknown, only for the love of their work, in places such as Bell Labs and General Electric's research and development facility in Schenectady, New York.

These unsung heroes change our lives every day. They are driven not by self-interest but by an insatiable urge to create, invent, improve, and discover—all for the common good.

The server's CVA is his charming, guileless manner (sometimes hidden behind a goofy smile or scraggly beard) that wins over the hearts of associates and fellow workers, eventually breaking down the defensive barriers of even the most committed curmudgeons and naysayers. Not surprisingly, servers tend to congregate more in nonprofit and volunteer organizations than in the private sector. When they rise to the top in the private sector—as Branson did—their ascendancy is not only noteworthy but often surprising.

THE SEER

The seer vaults across time and space to bring valued insight to the present. Perhaps more than those in other categories, the seer is held in the highest regard, because everybody loves a futurist. The seer rides the wave ahead of change, while the sage follows the seer and tries to massage change. Like the priest, the seer traffics in areas most of us are unwilling or unable to visit. Some seers, such as Lester Thurow, position themselves so far out on the economic time line—a hundred years—that few people will ever know if the predications are right.

The adventurous seer is always engrossing. He manages to capture credibility because he bases his conclusions on all that has come to pass up to this moment—then projects trend lines using computer models. The best seers, such as *Whole Earth Catalogue* founder, top management guru, Infonet pioneer, and futurist Stewart Brand, constantly challenge, stimulate, and confound. Brand takes the contrarian position, for example, that "hindsight is better than foresight. That's why revolutionary forms always work better than visionary designs. They grow from experience rather than from somebody's forehead." With hindsight, he develops "scenarios" that depict a business future of very strong likelihood. In 1973 Brand predicted the emergence of the PC—six years before Steven Jobs even started tinkering in his garage. And then there's Peter Drucker, who—even in his eighties—was still looking ahead. And Tom Peters borrows from the best minds in business to translate current emerging trends into a manageable future reality. This kind of thinking brings extra value to the table. That's why I always tell my clients that if they want to position themselves as leaders, they must understand the role of seers.

The seer's CVA in the Age of Knowledge is a glimpse of the future based on the seer's ability to interpret that future based on what he already knows of the past—and a willingness to make a projection that could be wrong.

THE COURTIER

The courtier may see himself as the power behind the throne. Courtiers function best not in the limelight, but still lit by its seductive glow. They are comfortable in second place, but if suddenly thrust upon the scene—as Harry Truman was upon the death of President Roosevelt—can prove to be surprisingly effective and decisive. On the other hand, some courtiers such as former secretary of state Alexander Haig, are forever looking to find ways to enlarge their power—but may not sit well upon the throne. Who can forget the curious scene as Haig marched, sweating, to the microphones after the failed assassination attempt on Ronald Reagan in 1982 and blurted at the TV cameras: "I'm in charge here!"? Much of the country, you may recall, viewed this strange scene with dismay. Most CEOs have trusted courtiers who may or may not be yes-men, depending on what kind of foil the CEO may be seeking.

Courtiers can also be partners—as in the relationship of Microsoft cofounders Bill Gates and Paul Allen, who today is very happy to stay out of Gates's way but who remains close to Gates and serves as an adviser and sounding board.

And some CEOs, such as Chuck Lee at GTE, have been courtiers themselves—but Lee, unlike most courtiers, quickly discarded his courtier coat to put on the mantles of coach and king. Courtiers labor long and faithfully in the vineyards, and like good monks, suddenly find themselves promoted to abbot. (Courtiers once thrived best in mature, quasi-monopolistic businesses like insurance and banking, where friendly boards rewarded their long years of service with constant promotion and eventual ascendancy to the top job.)

Today the courtier's role is under serious pressure. Boards are no longer necessarily friendly—fearing for their own safety in time of fiduciary scrutiny—and courtiers often find themselves out of work and looking for a new job. Paradoxically, they often land in rival companies and wind up as warriors leading one-time foes, now allies, against former employers.

The courtier's CVA is to provide honest counsel to the king (even if that counsel might bring unwelcome news), to help develop the corporate (or departmental) party line, and to speak for the king (boss or CEO) whenever circumstances prevent the king from speaking for himself.

The opera of life is full of colorful characters we meet every day. But each character's destiny is determined by how well he understands and uses CVA.

No one reading this book will likely see himself as a buffoon or a trickster. Certainly no one in business would admit to either. But there is a little bit of both in each of us. The desire to try to be funny, for example, when we aren't, or when laughter is inappropriate. The temptation to swagger or boast or brag. The temptation to grandstand and siphon credit from others. These things can bring us down.

The corporate leader hall of shame is littered with the painful memories of many a joke that bombed, many a remark that offended, and many a misrepresentation that boomeranged. Why take a risk when you can be a statesman, coach, or king? Common sense will always prevail over blind stabs at self-aggrandizement. If you see yourself as a buffoon, you will come across as a buffoon. If you see yourself as a king, you may well wind up something like a king.

In the film *Wall Street*, Gordon Gekko, played by Michael Douglas, was no buffoon, but he was a cynical trickster who would stop at nothing to get money and power. In his memorable "greed is good" speech, Gekko mesmerized an audience of perturbed investors with charm and a talent for distorting the truth. In the end, Gekko's house of cards collapsed and, not unlike a number of real-life Wall Street hustlers, he was driven to ruin.

The only way to find your true voice is to speak from the heart. If you care about what you are saying, the merchant or server or sage or coach inside you will emerge. Keep a lid on the buffoon or trickster. But for the rest, let them come out. Encourage them to come out. Then *become* that priest, that warrior, that king or coach. Let them all out and let them speak. You and your audiences will both profit from it.

> **The way to find your true voice is to speak from your heart.**

CHAPTER

EIGHTEEN

Choosing the High Road

The ultimate test of CVA lies in the answer to one very old question: Is it true that the word really is mightier than the sword?

Can one person move seas of people to action when battalions of armed soldiers might fail? The power of propaganda—artful political persuasion through deception and guile—is legendary, and advertising is an art form upon which much of the world's commerce depends. In America alone, advertisers spend more than $1 trillion every year just to make sure their products and services stay competitive. That's more than the gross national products of Canada, Denmark, and Chile combined.

Coca-Cola and Pepsi-Cola, for example, are little more than sugared water. Yet Coca-Cola is the world's most recognized brand, and Coke's stock has been a consistent winner through the years.

That's because Coke and Pepsi are not selling brown

soda. What they are selling, year after year at a cost of billions of advertising dollars, is youth, fun, and excitement.

Every government, including our own, serves up a soup of half-truths (propaganda) to its own citizens and to the world. For seventy years, the people of the Soviet Union lived the lie of communism—only to find themselves waking up unprepared for the challenges of a new world.

The powers of persuasion are all around us, in every ad, in every commercial on TV and radio, in every newspaper article and editorial, in every conversation in our private and professional lives. We are shaped by the 6,000 or so direct and subliminal stimuli *Advertising Age* says we absorb every day.

If the advertiser can control our minds so as to get his hand in our wallets, what power do we have as individuals to influence those around us? Do the same principles apply? If you write a good letter, you're likely to be even more effective on the phone. If you're good on the phone, you're probably at your best face-to-face.

Churchill, through his frequent radio broadcasts during the pivotal Battle of Britain, steeled a "nation of shopkeepers" to turn back the savage Nazi tide. British fighter pilots in their wooden Hurricanes successfully fought off the German Luftwaffe. It was a great moment in history. "Never have so many owed so much to so few," Churchill said, eulogizing his underdog British fliers after they prevailed against huge odds. Today many historians believe that one man and his words are the main reason people are not speaking German in London today.

Not only does the power of the spoken word hold sway over people's minds, but that same power also presents a wonderful opportunity to do the right thing.

Every time we open our mouths, and by inference, our minds, we have a choice. We can choose to help or to harm. To deceive or to tell the truth. We can choose to illuminate or to obfuscate. We can intimidate or give support, see the light or see the darkness. We can choose to search out the right or to ignore it. We can seek a higher good or just go on with business as usual.

Encouragement. Inspiration. Enlightenment. Help. Truth. Love. Compassion. Wisdom. All the values that every prophet and every religion have taught us since recorded time began.

In business as well as in our private lives, we can choose to color all that we do—and ultimately what we say, which defines who we are—with a greater good.

The greater good could be nothing more than serving the client as we ourselves would want to be served—with conscience, consideration, and dedication.

Every time we open our mouths, we have a choice.

That good service to the client (or the audience) can manifest itself in many ways: knowing your message, then delivering it well; being brief yet complete; providing lots

181

of examples; beginning strongly and ending strongly; speaking in a conversational way; and absolutely refusing to bore the people who are obligated to listen to you.

At the very least, even though we may not feel able to be saintly or save the world, we should try to be interesting.

Have a quarterly report due to the operating committee? Give extra value (CVA). Help the operating committee get more than it may expect by first *projecting* future sales, market share, and other performance indicators. In other words, start with the future. That's the interesting part—your read on what's coming and what we ought to be doing to make it happen. *Then* go back and talk about the last quarter, but only as a way to offer evidence of what you see coming.

Got an assignment to speak to a trade group about upgrading steam generators? A purely technical walk-through will have limited appeal to an audience that may know as much about generators as you do. How about starting with that videotape in your drawer that shows the mangled remains of a generator that was serviced improperly? Follow the tape with a series of short personal vignettes relating your own experience in the pits and buckets of great machines gone wrong because of human inattentiveness. Then tell them your theme: An ounce of prevention is worth a pound of cure. You might even remind them of that motor oil TV ad in which the pitchman stands amid a heap of discarded cars in a junkyard and leers at the camera, saying, "You can see me now—or you can see me later." Then ask them, "When was the last time you ran a cost analysis on service and repair?" Tell them that machines are like people. The older you are, the more likely you are to get sick. Regular checkups are required, with remedial steps taken as needed. A potential catastrophic failure inside a power generation system is *not* like prostate cancer. Watchful waiting is not advised.

Then just keep on trucking.

The more personal, more human, more interesting your story, the greater the service to your audience. If you take the view that it is in the interest of everyone—customers, municipalities, employees, shareholders—to maintain and upgrade equipment regularly, then we have also risen to the level of the greater good.

By contrast, the lowest disservice we can render is to lie. Ironically, though, that's exactly what a lot of people in public office apparently do much of the time. One reason the vigilante militia leaders say they gained so much momentum in the United States is because political leaders often pledge less government interference in our lives before they're elected, then do the opposite after they're voted in.

The more personal and interesting your story, the greater your service to the audience.

In our time, many a politician has gotten elected on the promise of lower taxes—only to go back on that promise after election. Politicians counter by claiming that if they told the truth all the time, no one would ever get elected and there would be no one to run the government.

Frankly, they may have a point. And there is evidence that a number of honest candidates who did tell it like it is, never got past the primaries.

But in a recent poll a large majority of Americans said they would tell the truth if they had been the candidate. (Do you believe that?) People say they feel it is the duty of their elected representatives to be honest.

The point is that we all want to expect the truth from others. Yet when we hear the outright truth, we treat it as an event. Truth is news.

Congressman Tim LeBoutellier (R., NY) told me that the reason he was not elected to a second term is because he always insisted on telling the truth—even the ugly, painful truth—both privately to his peers, and publicly to his constituents and the media. In telling the truth he put what he felt were the long-term interests of his constituents and his country ahead of his own.

The irony: Long-term perspective can mean a short-term term of office.

Presidents Carter and Clinton have both been quoted as lamenting upon the sometimes career-threatening nature of truth-telling in public policy.

Many a great man has gone to his death noting that in the end our only real worth, the only value we can take with us into the next world, is our honor—that is, the quality of the character we build in our lifetimes and measure by the strength of our integrity.

Given that definition of the value of the truth, we would be fools not to prize and cultivate it in ourselves.

In business we can quickly seize on false honesty when a corporate leader declaims about the issue under discussion, "It's not the money, it's the principle!" Then you know it's time to check your pockets and head for the door. Or when a big kahuna intones, "My friends, I want to be honest with you." Tell us, uh, friend, what were you being the rest of the time? Or when a local squire tells you how much he misses the hellish days he once spent in a summer job stoking the roaring furnace of a steel mill. He tells you this little story during his speech at a champagne fund-raiser in the Hamptons.

Sometimes businesspeople become desensitized to reality from years of listening to the drumbeat of their own party line. Corporate leaders wind up telling half-truths and outright falsehoods that sound like they were written by the company flack—which they probably were.

Just listen to these portions of separate *Fortune* interviews with outgoing Sears CEO Ed Brennan and incoming Sears chief Arthur Martinez:

Fortune: Has Sears' target customer changed?

Brennan: No. Not really. The customer who buys appliances or lawn mowers from us covers a very broad economic spectrum.

Martinez: Yes. Strange as it may sound, nobody in the company really understood who was shopping in the departments, who was making the purchase decisions. In almost every case it was the woman in the family. And we didn't seem to care very much about her. . . .

Fortune: How did Sears' image suffer, particularly a

few years ago when the automotive centers got blasted for overcharging for repairs?

Brennan: We never lost the goodwill of the American consumer. The automotive situation was a temporary blow to the automotive business. Interestingly, it never rubbed off on the balance of the store.

Martinez: I got here two or three months after the automotive thing broke. I underestimated what a profound potential breakdown in trust it represented. It clearly impacted how people thought about the store. In general, our brand perception with consumers still has a long way to go.

Fortune: In a 1993 cover story called "The Dinosaurs," *Fortune* described the declines of Sears, IBM, and General Motors. Was Sears a dinosaur?

Brennan: The article lumped the three corporations together. I think that wasn't fair, based on what we were doing at the time. I mean, we were making huge changes.

Martinez: . . . I don't think the reporting was inaccurate at all. The word "dinosaur" implies that the company will eventually become extinct. There was a real risk of that, I think, at the time the article was written. . . .

Fortune: Was the financial supermarket (Allstate, Dean Witter) a mistake?

Brennan: It wasn't a mistake. . . .

Martinez: We're not going to re-create the financial supermarket. . . .

Fortune: Rate Sears' recent management.

Brennan: My peers and I have had one of the larger

business challenges of the past fifty years. We came out the other side in great shape. . . .

Martinez: . . . When I came in, the organization was impatient for leadership. People wanted strategic direction. . . .

What we have here is not an absence of truth, or even a distortion of truth, but rather the *perception* of truth as advanced by two individuals under the same roof and in the same job. But one of these men is more truthful—if truth can be measured by candor and honesty—than the other. Yet this is not to say that Ed Brennan is dishonest. He certainly is not. But it is clear just listening to both men talk that Ed is unable to see things as they are, or is at least unwilling to *admit* he can see things as they are. By contrast, Martinez is disarmingly straightforward. His fresh approach flies in the face of corporate tradition, represented by the outgoing CEO. In a sense, Martinez is the new, tell-it-like-it-is voice of the twenty-first century, while Brennan speaks with the tongue of a spinmeister and echoes the public-relations culture of the twentieth century. Martinez' candor characterizes his style, one that goes a long way to breeding confidence and trust, not only among the MTV-bred, fundamentally distrustful next generation of Sears' customers but also among the media, Wall Street, shareholders, and employees. It is no surprise that Sears' board picked Martinez, and not another brainwashed Sears insider, to lead Sears over the top.

People will drop their guard and embrace you if you appear to be making an effort to tell the truth. But get caught lying—in a speech, on the air, or in newspapers or magazines—and be prepared to suffer the consequences.

Even a little lie can boomerang to give you a bloody nose.

American Airlines had to pay a $500,000 penalty instead of the standard $600 lost luggage fee because a judge ruled the airline had misrepresented a lost bag circumstance with a vacationing passenger. The bag didn't show up for nine days, even though the airline repeatedly promised it would be at the passenger's hotel the next morning. The judge punished the airline not for losing the bag but for failing to tell the truth.

> **People will embrace you and what you have to say if you make a sincere effort to tell the truth.**

Truth in advertising has become a hot—and sometimes sore—topic. (To make sure advertising claims don't get too far out of line, the Food and Drug Administration and the Federal Communications Commission "help" ad people resist the temptation to dodge the truth or misrepresent facts.)

The Truth in Information Act has exposed false claims, and set new standards and expectations for anyone who can read a newspaper or watch television.

Full disclosure is also a welcome policy for anyone who has to buy a house or sign a contract.

In spite of occasional rumblings such as repeated

charges that the tobacco industry has for years hidden from the public the dangers of smoking, business ethics have never been better. In fact, ethics—measured in part by candor and truthfulness—are today an asset worth more than a whole year's advertising budget.

For example, it took an oil spill to transform Ashland Oil from a company with a shadowy presence in the public eye to a corporate good guy—almost overnight. With the Allegheny River polluted with oil and Pittsburgh without a water supply, the company responded quickly. The chairman went to the microphones and said something like: "This is a mistake. It's our fault. We're very sorry, but we're fixing the problem. And when we fix the problem, we will exceed all federal, state, and local requirements so you can be sure it won't ever happen again."

Bingo. Harmful news story suddenly a harmless non-story and vanishing from page one to a small item in the back of the local newspapers the next day. Conversely, had the chairman chosen to stonewall, obfuscate, be defensive, point fingers, refuse to accept responsibility, fail to show remorse, or refuse to meet with reporters—which is what everyone was expecting—he would have failed to hit a pubic relations grand slam. Instead, he might have wound up in a bitter, ugly national spitting match that could have dragged on for months and been as harmful as the frank and open approach was helpful.

This was a happy ending for Ashland, but a lesson not learned by giant rival Exxon, which could have avoided an image-spoiling goof if they had only been paying attention. After the now-famous oil spill in Alaska that fouled one of the most pristine places on earth, Exxon's chairman didn't say a word or show his face for five tense days—while an angry public waited for signs of leadership and an appropriate response. When he finally did show his face, it was pretty much the same old corporate double-speak. Plus, Exxon's emergency response was slow, poorly coordinated, and seemed to lack real commitment. Worse, Americans felt like they couldn't trust Exxon to keep us informed and tell the truth.

It was a bad moment for Exxon. And even now, years later, they still haven't recovered from that PR setback.

Telling the truth is a better choice—for strictly practical reasons. The truth is attractive. The truth is courageous. And the truth is more interesting than a lie.

Most importantly, you can't have CVA without candor. In business, a consistent reputation for truthfulness is money in the bank—and a leader with a reputation for anything less than honesty is a leader in name only.

> **Next to quality, most audiences—particularly business audiences—prize nothing more than brevity.**

CHAPTER
NINETEEN

The Silent Partner: A Surprising Source of Creativity

The chairman of an international oil company once confided to me that after some of his fellow board members complained that his public appearances were underwhelming, he started saying "a little prayer" before each speaking event. Pretty soon, he said, he found he was overflowing with new ideas that were not only flavoring the speeches but actually helping to shape the business itself.

The head of R&D for a major manufacturing company, a man of impeccable international scientific credentials, told me that his best ideas came not in the shower but after periods of meditation.

The president of a midsize high-tech firm says he relies on the managerial gifts of inspiration, right thinking, and mental discipline gained from years of practicing Zen Buddhism to map strategy and set goals in his growing business.

All these people discovered for themselves a spiritual element in business that they never learned in business school.

It took me years to wake up to the missing piece in my own working life—the possibilities of spiritual potential in business.

This is another aspect of CVA.

My first glimpse of this elusive element of CVA came in a large room years ago. I can remember as a boy wandering into my great-aunt's sculpture studio and marveling at the clay and stone taking shape all around me. Everywhere was the fruit of her hands, her creative fire transforming the stuff of the earth. It was like a strange garden of half-born creatures under a skylight almost as big as the sky itself.

I heard a voice in the shadows. My great-aunt appeared near a cluster of large bronze circus figures—clowns, acrobats, elephants—that she had recently had cast for an upcoming show.

She seemed swathed in gloom, like a statue herself. I thought she looked large and menacing.

"How do you make them look so real?" I asked. She moved slowly toward me, seemingly surprised by the question. She thought about it for a moment and then said very simply, "I just pray. Before I begin working, I always pray."

I was confused. Pray?

"Why?" I asked.

She wasn't comfortable with my question, but she tried to answer me. "Because I need help. I can't do all this by myself. Nobody can. We all need help in every-thing we do," she said.

I still didn't understand.

"What happens when you pray?" I asked.

"It's as if there's a special energy out there, and when I pray it comes to me. It's as if that energy wants to help me create—but first I have to *invite* it to come."

She could see I wasn't getting it.

"How do you know it likes to help you create?" I de-manded. She just looked at me and smiled, suddenly at a loss. "I just know," she whispered, as if she were letting me in on a secret.

It wasn't until much later that I had an inkling of what she was talking about. And now that I think I understand, I often remember that moment in the studio so long ago.

"I just pray," she said.

I don't pray in the sense that we often think of prayer.

I'm not talking about prayer in the deeply religious sense of the word. But, odd as it may sound, I am talking about "extra" or internal communication that can help make things happen. I see myself in league with invisible business partners who will help if I "invite" them to. I discovered this truth simply by trying it out. I asked for help on several occasions and—to my surprise—was never disappointed.

I can remember a number of lectures, seminars, and private sessions in which a strange transformation seemed to occur that was entirely beyond my control. I would be in the middle of a lecture and suddenly several things would happen at once: I would "jump" up to another level of clarity, feel a surge of energy, a diffusion with new insights, and experience a combustion of creativity not unlike an afterburner kicking in on a jet engine.

Could it be that this was the same phenomenon my great-aunt had described to me years before?

Ask for help—you'll probably get it.

One of the most startling characteristics of this "altered state," if you will, is the distinctly curious sensation that your consciousness is dividing into two separate entities, even as you speak. On occasion I have found myself gaining momentum, then flying along bolstered by a surge of inspiration welling up inside. In this transition I mentally separate from myself and become another member of the audience—a witness to my own performance. I am not out of my body. I still see through the same eyes. And I am not hovering near the ceiling. But now I am both spectator and speaker, unlike everyone else in the room. And I seem to be the only person who knows what is happening to me.

All of this bears mentioning because it has to do with a part of CVA that we can only access by asking for help. The best reason to ask for help is to deliver better quality. If you fulfill your role as a speaker, then you are positioning yourself as a leader—a person with ideas, a plan, an opinion, a solution, something worth listening to. You teach, you enlighten, you guide and explain. That's what leaders do. And if you are in the business of teaching (which most people, whether they know it or not, are), then there is much more you can learn so you may better teach, better enlighten. That's why I think it makes sense to ask for help—even if you suspect there's nobody listening on the other end of the line.

I thought there couldn't possibly be anyone actually listening. Then experience proved me wrong. Now I'm convinced that there *is* someone on the other end of the line—an invisible partner happy to heed my call and pitch in to help me be the best I can be, not for my own sake, but for the sake of the people who count on me to deliver quality and value.

> **Teach. Enlighten. Guide. Explain. That's what leaders do.**

Interestingly, the help I ask for does not always kick in until I need it most—for example, in a speech or seminar at the end of an exhausting workweek when I have been in five cities in five days. The tank is practically empty, I'm flying on vapors, and my brain is on overload. I feel a little like Jean Valjean on the Paris barricades in *Les Misérables*: One more day, I'm thinking, just one day more. . . .

This is the unhappy state I found myself in on Friday afternoon at the Aspen Institute, where I was running a symposium for senior officers of a big corporation. About halfway into the three-hour meeting I wasn't sure I'd have the juice to make it through the balance of the day. The job required me to talk for most of the three hours, and as the afternoon grew longer I began to worry that quality might suffer.

I asked for a little help to give these good people the value they expected and deserved.

I didn't have to worry long. Soon I began to feel like a new person. My mind cleared. I began to relax. I felt refreshed and renewed. And then that strange duality set in. Now I was a silent witness, marveling as someone else seemed to be putting just the right words in my mouth.

I was two people. One person was speaking. The other person—detached, fascinated—was listening. Yet both these people coexisted simultaneously inside the same body. In a way I may never understand, I believe that this phenomenon is linked to someone listening on the other end of the line.

Prayer. Asking for help. Meditation. These are forms of communication to a source of power we can only guess at. Even if you see yourself as a nuts-and-bolts, eminently practical person who has no truck with things metaphysical, you have nothing to lose by asking for a little help with your next speech or presentation. Of course, you can ask for help (From God? From yourself? From the cosmos? It doesn't matter) with other matters—and you'll probably get it—but you may see the quickest and most recognizable rewards with an occasion that requires you to speak or to lead.

The greatest sin is to bore your audience.

CHAPTER
TWENTY

The Last Word

Why does any of this matter?

It matters because we are living in unsettled times and each of us needs all the help we can get. We've all been affected—not always happily—by the events of recent years. Fairness has nothing to do with it. Seismic changes have left a lot of very good people on the beach. For those people and others still trying to navigate dangerous seas, now is the time to take charge of your life. If you feel helpless, now is the time to decide your destiny. Right now is the time to control events, rather than allowing events to control you.

In the future, opportunity lies in articulation. Practitioners who have not forgotten the speaking game and how to play it will fare well. In a world of data dumping, channel surfing, computer addiction, and digital miracles of all kinds, people will value more than they ever dreamed those who can lead, inspire, and motivate.

> **People who speak well will flourish in the years ahead.**

So if you intend to be a part of this evolving future world, you owe it to yourself to prepare yourself to be a leader, no matter how big or how small your world—and whatever your role or whatever your rank. If you happen to be a student, make sure that when you sign up for Computer Science 103, you also take a course in debating or public speaking.

Just look at what's going on:

The dawn of the Age of Knowledge has generated unprecedented upheaval and anxiety. With downsizing, reorganization, consolidations, mergers, acquisitions, and reengineering, some 3.5 million white-collar workers found themselves out of jobs in just a few years. Worse, the jobs themselves disappeared. Whole tiers of management, departments, even divisions simply went away—never to come back.

The result: Shell-shocked survivors are now being asked to do the work of all those people who had been let go. Larger workload. Longer hours. For the first time, the function of leadership was being pushed down through the ranks, so that today more people than ever before are being asked to head teams, projects, special assignments, and work groups.

Those who wound up on the outside looking in—many out of work for the first time in their lives—had to find a way to earn a living. Many recast themselves as experts, consulting for the very companies that had cut them loose.

What this adds up to is a new working environment in which leadership—or the perception of leadership—is a powerful piece of currency. Now people see the element of leadership as essential to any long-term business relationship. The CFO wants to know that the thirty-eight-year-old investment banker sitting across from him is a leader. The vice president wants to know that the sales rep for his biggest vendor can also consult, advise, and counsel—can head a partnership group to find a solution. The plant manager wants to know that her top engineer can effectively lead and manage a new product development team.

The perception of leadership is a powerful piece of currency.

The Age of Knowledge, for all its vaunted technical communications wizardry, will still require brainpower and word power. As the Great Flood of Innovation washes over us, it will still fall to just folks to provide explanation, inspiration, interpretation, illumination, exposition, articulation, and especially translation. We will all have to translate and interpret mountains of data and information to create knowledge. We will generate knowledge like never before, have access to knowledge like never before, and consequently be in danger of knowledge overwhelming us.

> **We will all have to translate and interpret mountains of data and information.**

So *The Articulate Executive* and *The Inspired Executive* are for all those brave souls everywhere who will journey together, as Bill Gates says, "On the Road Ahead." As our world becomes more technical, we've got to become more articulate. As our world tuns faceless, we've go to emerge as more distinct, more human. As technology quickens and business reinvents itself every few years, each of us must be prepared to step forward, unleash our CVA, and begin to make things happen. Together we've got to design and build the world of complex human and informational interactions we all will share—and a world in which the articulate will rise to opportunity.

Index

Interesting, being, 17–18, 32, 35, 92–93, 182, 196
Interpersonal relationships, xvii, 56

Jobs, Steven, 62, 63, 173
John Paul II, Pope, 83

Kearns, David, 136
Kennedy, John F., 122
Kerr, Steven, 8
Kiam, Victor, 12
King, 159, 160, 161, 166–67, 176
Kissinger, Henry, 163
Knowledge
  Age of, xiv-xvi, 51, 174, 198, 199
  inspirational, 128
Koresh, David, 59

Lawyers, focused thought on, 137
Layoffs, downsizing and, 53–55, 137, 198–99
Leaders
  characteristics of, 35–36
  as currency, 199
  decency and, 151–57
  doing the right things, 151–57
  downsizing and, 198
  focus and, 140
  prayers as help for, 191–96
  preparation for, 198
  satori achieved by, 102
  as teachers, 38, 194–95
  visual aids avoided by, 94
Leadership positioning, 91, 92
Leadership roles, 159–78
  buffoon, 159, 160, 162–63, 176
  coach, 159, 161, 170–71
  courtier, 159, 161, 174–77
  king, 159, 160, 161, 166–67, 176
  merchant, 159, 160
  priest, 159, 164–65
  sage, 159, 161, 163–64
  seer, 159, 161, 173–74
  server, 159, 161, 171–72
  statesman, 159, 161
  trickster, 159, 160–61, 160–62, 168–69, 176
  warrior, 159, 160, 169–70
Lebenthal, Mort, 12
LeBoutellier, Tim, 184

Lee, Chuck, 175
Lies, truths versus, 183–90
Likability, 28
  see also Business likability
Lincoln, Abraham, 49–50
Lombardi, Vince, 128

McDougal, Jim, 169
Mack, John, 108–9
McNealy, Scott, 136
Managerial role, anecdote on, 124–25
Managers
  communicating urgency of message to, 63–64, 65
  doing things right, 154–55
Market Value Added (MVA), 5–6
Martinez, Arthur, 166, 185–87
Mediocrity, 89
Meditation, creativity from, 191–96
Merchant, 159, 160
Message
  anecdote as, 119–20
  communicating urgency of, 63–64, 65
  more than one, 146
  personal delivery of, 110
  speaking inseparable from, 8
  see also Theme
Meyer, Fred, Inc., 71
Michelangelo, 101–2
Mickey Mouse rules, anecdote on, 122–23
Microsoft, 10, 63, 80, 141–42, 159, 175
Miller, Robert, 71
Missionary-style, urgency of message conveyed by, 65
Mizner, Wilson, 138
Money, focused thought on, 138
Mouth, connecting to brain, 75–81, 89–90
Mozart, Wolfgang Amadeus, 102
Murray, Jim, 128–29
Mussolini, Benito, 159, 162

National Association of College and Employers (NACE), xvii
National Enquirer, 109
Newman, Paul, 85
Nixon, Richard, 92, 163